A N
I N D E P E N D E N T
W O M A N

 AN INDEPENDENT

WOMAN ■ *The Autobiography*

of EDITH GUERRIER

Edited with an introduction by Molly Matson

Foreword by Polly Welts Kaufman

The University of Massachusetts Press

AMHERST ————————————————————

Copyright © 1992 by
The University of Massachusetts Press
All rights reserved
Printed in the United States of America
LC 91-18499
ISBN 0-87023-756-X
Designed by Mary Mendell
Set in Janson Text by Keystone Typesetting, Inc.
Printed and bound by Thomson-Shore, Inc.

Library of Congress Cataloging in Publication Data
Guerrier, Edith, 1870–1958.
An independent woman : the autobiography of
Edith Guerrier / edited with an introduction by
Molly Matson ; foreword by Polly Welts Kaufman.
p.   cm.
Includes bibliographical references and index.
ISBN 0–87023–756–X (alk. paper)
1. Guerrier, Edith. 1870–1958. 2. Librarians—
United States—Biography. 3. Women social
reformers—United States—Biography.
4. Feminists—United States—Biography.
I. Matson, Molly. II. Title.
Z720.G89A3   1992
020'.92—dc20
[B]   91–18499 CIP
This book is published with the support and
cooperation of the University of Massachusetts at
Boston
British Library Cataloguing in Publication data are
available.

For
Lucy, Kate, Martha,
and their father

CONTENTS

ILLUSTRATIONS

Polly Welts Kaufman

 The autobiography of Edith Guerrier illustrates in one woman's life how the response of women to the multiple disruptions of society of the late nineteenth century combined with new opportunities to produce the "New Woman" of the early twentieth century. Often out of economic necessity, new women replaced traditional family roles of wife, mother, or spinster aunt with improvised careers in new fields. The availability of higher education for thousands of young women, representing nearly 37 percent of college students by the turn of the century, led to lifelong careers for many women, not just temporary jobs designed to fill the time between school and marriage.[1]

The new woman who, like Edith Guerrier, chose to remain single also created a new kind of family unconnected by ties of kinship. Made up of pairs of women linked in "Boston marriages" or groups of self-supporting women living together in lasting relationships, these surrogate families offered the economic and emotional support for women once provided by traditional families.[2] With woman's culture as its base, Edith Guerrier's life path intersected many of the most creative attempts to counter the forces of immigration, urbanization, and industrialization that destabilized the existing society.

Although she participated in the earnest efforts to Americanize the individuals arriving in the high tide of immigration from eastern Europe, Guerrier wanted to give them more than just survival skills. After a stint as an aid in the nursery schools supported by philanthropist Pauline Agassiz Shaw, she was assigned to conduct girls' clubs in several settlement houses and at Shaw's North Bennet Street Industrial School in Boston's North End, where Guerrier also maintained a reading room and a Boston Public Library book delivery station. Demonstrating the empathy that was to make her such a durable role model for the girls and young women from the Jewish and Italian families who crowded the North End, Guerrier wanted to do more than just "keep the girls off the street," but she did not know how. She turned to improvisation, reasoning, "I know life has far more to offer than I have yet found. Undoubtedly these girls feel the same way about it. Perhaps we can find together the key to some secret garden in which we can profitably enjoy ourselves" (p. 68). [3]

Taking her cues from their responses, Edith Guerrier soon began to share her love of literature and gaiety through storytelling and plays, dramatizing folktales, or writing new scripts herself. Her programs grew until they were divided into afternoon and evening groups for girls of all ages, reserving Saturday evenings for the oldest group, who continued to meet and call itself the Saturday Evening Girls, even after the members started their own careers. Their activities grew more sophisticated over time and included operettas and a performance in Isabella Stewart Gardner's Museum. Although Guerrier's programs fell far short of genuine multiculturalism, she did accept such "immigrant gifts" as folk dancing and had at least one of her plays translated so it could be performed in Italian. [4]

Guerrier's work with the girls' clubs led to her lifelong career in the new field for women of librarianship. Always viewing libraries as dedicated to social service, she was among the women who changed the direction of library service to include children's rooms and storytelling, so popular that three years after the first children's room in the Boston Public Library opened in 1895, it had to be doubled in size. [5] Impressed with Guerrier's library clubs, Helen Osborne Storrow, a member of both the board of the North Bennet Street Industrial School and of the Board of Visitors of the Boston Public Library, became their financial supporter in what soon became a branch library under Guerrier's direction. Guerrier eventually became the first woman supervisor of branch libraries, one of the top jobs in the Boston Public Library. As a federal worker during the First World War, she pioneered the distribution of information from government bulletins to public libraries. Like other new women she had improvised a career by opening up the possibilities inherent in a new field. [6]

Another characteristic of the new woman expressed in the life of

Edith Guerrier was her love of physical activity and belief in its restorative value. With the first money she ever earned as a teenager reading copy at the Riverside Press in Cambridge (where she also "inhaled" her love of books), she bought a "tennis set" of four rackets, a net, and balls. She took them with her to the Vermont Methodist Seminary and Female College at Montpelier, where she spent four happy years among the "encircling mountains," climbing Camel's Hump and playing baseball "vigorously" each fall and skating and tobogganing in the winter. An inveterate walker, she and Edith Brown, her partner for nearly forty years, who had come to Boston from Nova Scotia, thought nothing of following the shore on foot around Cape Ann from Annisquam to Gloucester in one day, a distance of twenty-five miles. Whether she influenced the decision or not is unknown, but Guerrier gave her full support to Helen Storrow's plan to build a camp at Wingaersheek Beach in West Gloucester where the girls from the clubs could spend two weeks away from the overcrowded North End in the summer, enjoying activities and eating meals they themselves planned with the help of a woman camp director.[7]

Edith Guerrier's response to the ethos of industrialization that sacrificed decent working conditions to profits and saw the worker as an extension of the machine was to join with Edith Brown to develop a pottery where the young women workers were valued as much, if not more, than their products. Named the Paul Revere Pottery after its original location in the North End on Hull Street, a few doors up from the Old North Church and next to the Copp's Hill Burying Ground, it is the pottery for which Guerrier, Brown, and the Saturday Evening Girls themselves are most known today.

The pottery idea was born on one of their marathon walks, this time in Switzerland, where Guerrier and Brown discussed the need for the girls in the library clubs to earn money for their two weeks in West Gloucester. Because they had been admiring the "charming peasant ware" all over Europe, they hit on the idea of starting an "art pottery" to give the club girls employment. Their plan was influenced by the values of John Ruskin and especially William Morris as expressed in the Arts and Crafts movement. The movement's goal was to bring back the sense of community that members believed had been destroyed by industrialization. They hoped to elevate the place of crafts and their creators in society and to bring beauty to household objects and restore a respect for labor.[8]

Although both Guerrier and Brown studied at the School of the Boston Museum of Fine Arts and Brown was teaching drawing at the North Bennet Street Industrial School, neither of them knew anything about making pottery. As new women, used to improvising their own lives, their lack of experience did not deter them then, as it had not before. They perfected their skills in the basement of their home with the help of girls from the library clubs. They asked the question, "Are modern conditions such that order, beauty, and happiness of daily living cannot be part of the shop as well as part of the home?" and they began to dream of a "little pottery in a garden where flowers would bloom from April to November, and where from November to April in warm, well-lighted rooms the girls would work happily at their benches" (p. 86).[9]

Convinced that the pottery would offer worthwhile and dignified employment to the young women, and still wanting to encourage the library clubs, Helen Storrow bought the Hull Street building for a library clubhouse and the pottery in 1908. Guerrier and Brown became "settled" in an apartment on the top floor. Guerrier became director of the girls' clubs, now numbering nine, including five evening groups of high-school girls named for their meeting days; and Brown became director of the pottery. The Saturday Evening Girls added a newspaper to their activities. Guerrier also continued her duties at the branch library.[10]

In 1915 Guerrier and Brown achieved their dream of "a pottery in a garden" with girls working in "warm, well-lighted rooms." Backed by Storrow, they designed and built an L-shaped two-story pottery in the style of an English country house, where they also lived, often with other women, on the top of Nottingham Hill in the Brighton section of Boston. Reached by walking up eighty steps from the Commonwealth Avenue streetcar, the pottery employed about two hundred women over time as well as offering classes until it closed at the beginning of World War II. The women worked an eight-hour day, long before the forty-hour week became standard even for women, and earned ten dollars a week. They listened to a reader while they produced tableware, vases, and bowls generally designed by Edith Brown until her death in 1932. Each piece was signed with the decorator's own initials and those of their club, "SEG." Pottery was sold through the SEG Bowl Shop in downtown Boston, staffed by club members, and also sold privately to Storrow's acquaintances. Pieces were shown at the exhibitions of Boston's Society of Arts and Crafts. The library clubs continued as well, meeting in their own club rooms in the new North End branch library, where Guerrier was in charge.[11]

Although the founders of the library clubhouse and the Paul Revere Pottery shared some characteristics with the settlement house workers and other women reformers of the time, their goals were quite different. Like the residents of Denison House, a woman-run settlement in the South End, Guerrier and Brown did live in the community they served for seven years, but theirs was a more genteel and personal model. Unlike Denison House, whose residents tried to meet the everyday needs of immigrant families and working women, the library clubhouse was open only to young, unmarried Jewish and Italian women who were in school or beginning to work. Their goals were entirely cultural and they served only females. An attempt to include boys in one afternoon group was not successful. Instead of helping working women demand better conditions in their jobs by helping them organize or join trade unions as the Women's Trade Union League did, Guerrier and Brown, with Storrow's essential assistance, created alternative work for women on an almost utopian plan.[12]

The women philanthropists who made Guerrier's work in the North End possible also represented different points of view. Pauline Agassiz Shaw worked to change existing institutions and was instrumental in introducing kindergartens and manual training classes to the Boston public schools. She became an important financial supporter of woman's suffrage, funding the Boston Equal Suffrage Association for Good Government, a new organization working for suffrage in order to increase the power of women reformers. On the other hand, Helen Osborne Storrow chose the separatist route. Instead of attempting to reform existing institutions, she supported new ones. In addition to sponsoring the Paul Revere Pottery and the library clubs, she brought the Girl Scouts to Boston and was the principal founder of the Women's City Club. Her husband, James Jackson Storrow, a political reformer, was not enthusiastic about woman's suffrage and she may have agreed; other women of her class thought that most women were not yet sufficiently educated to become good voters.[13] Although we do not know if Guerrier worked for suffrage, we do know that the Saturday Evening Girls supported it, noting later that they were "indoctrinated" at Shaw's North Bennet Street Industrial School.[14] Both Shaw and Storrow were new women, too, instituting and directing their philanthropies on their own.

Although she always expected to be called "Miss Guerrier," Edith Guerrier developed a more empathetic relationship with the young women she served than many social reformers in the Progressive movement. Her connection with the women from the library clubs was a genuine one and lasted long after most of them ceased to meet on a regular basis. She followed their careers, watching several of the young women become teachers, librarians, executive secretaries, or social workers. Many attended Simmons College, a new college founded with a goal of training women for new careers. The women who married became active in philanthropies themselves. On Guerrier's eightieth birthday the Saturday Evening Girls, who continued to meet until 1969, contributed to a library fund named in her honor.[15]

When Storrow asked Guerrier to become director of the library clubhouse, Guerrier rejected the impulse of "doing good." She remembered her insight into her motives when she met her first group of boys in a settlement house. Poor herself at the time, she believed she had been looking for "self-respect by assuming a position of authority toward those who were supposedly worse off than I was." She accepted the position at the library clubhouse because it was *not* "doing good." She saw it as a place where she and the young women working together would gain "practice in thinking" and learn "the value of cooperation" (p. 88).

Guerrier realized that her own life experience had been her best preparation. "Sometimes on winter evenings when I pass the cold corners where I waited for streetcars," she said, "I thank God that I had the real adventure of being ill-clad, ill-fed, ill-sheltered." She concluded, "I am grateful for this experience, which makes it easier for me to get the point of view of the girl who is literally on her own" (p. 69). It was her example as a new woman not dependent on anyone else for economic support that she presented to be emulated.

Undoubtedly Edith Guerrier's unusual childhood kept her from trying to exercise social control over the young Jewish and Italian women of the North End by limiting their aspirations to practical goals. Instead, she wanted each woman to experience high culture. Guerrier's childhood and youth were filled with so many discontinuities in location, social class, and economic level that the only conclusion she could have reached was that achieving quality of life was up to her and, by extension, that any young woman's future lay in her own hands. In recounting her childhood "adventures," as she called them, Guerrier used a storybook style reminiscent of the tale of Lucy Larcom and other girls' stories of the downward mobility of the deserving poor who earn back their proper places in society because of the strength of their characters.[16] Her childhood story is the most compelling part of her autobiography.

Edith Guerrier was three when her mother died, and from that time until she entered the Vermont Methodist Seminary and Female College at the age of sixteen, her father moved her back and forth with no advance warning between her mother's comfortable family in New Bedford, where an aunt and uncle adored her, and the stern, poor family of her father's uncle, a Methodist minister living in various parishes in southern New England. In between and just before she went to Vermont, her father, a Civil War veteran, tried to make a home for her, first in Concord and then on the Kansas prairie at the edge of the Santa Fe Trail, where one summer she counted "seventy-six covered wagons passing our door." She described a "glorious" adventure with a "cowgirl" on borrowed horses where she felt real freedom—"the horse and I seemed motionless while the sky rushed by above us and the earth raced backward under our feet" (p. 46). Dismayed by her adventure, her father decided she should return East to school.

From the time Guerrier migrated to Boston in 1891 and began her career until her father's death in 1911, Guerrier, like most women of her time, was subject to the "family claim." Almost as soon as her father gave up the struggle of trying to make a home for her, she took on the task of trying to make a home for him, which became increasingly difficult as he declined in health and spirits. Her search for home finally ended in 1915 with the building of the Paul Revere Pottery on Nottingham Hill. There she stayed until her death more than forty years later.[17]

The new woman who appeared in American society at the turn of the century was created by the uncertainties of a rapidly changing world and a half century of public demands for "women's emancipation." Both young women of native stock who migrated to the city from declining farms and young women immigrants from Nova Scotia and Europe found themselves on their own. They could not depend on families with limited incomes to support them, nor did they always see marriage as a viable economic solution. Thrown on their own with only a few careers open to them, they accepted the help of the women who came before them, who founded or supported such organizations as Boston's YWCA, the North Bennet Street Industrial School, the Women's Educational and Industrial Union, the Women's Trade Union League, or Denison House. Women often passed on the help they received to the next generation of women. Edith Guerrier's life story is an example of women improvising a new kind of life for women as they networked across social class and among ethnic groups, together defining their lives and insuring their survival with style—bread *and* roses—in a new world.

My attention first settled on Edith Guerrier as I was casting about for a topic that might interest a group of university women whose monthly luncheon meeting I had been asked to address. The subject of her work with a settlement house group called the Saturday Evening Girls and their Paul Revere Pottery, recently the focus of an excellent exhibit on the campus of the University of Massachusetts–Boston, soon suggested itself as a rather attractive possibility. I had seen the exhibit and was delighted to learn that the major source of energy fueling the SEG and their pottery was a woman who was, as I am, a librarian. I was equally delighted to discover that someone I knew, the wife of a professor of psychology at the university, was the daughter of one of the Girls and had been, as I soon found out, the inspiration for the exhibit. I decided to speak about the Saturday Evening Girls and Edith Guerrier.

I gave my little talk, then put away my notes and bibliography with the semiformulated intention of someday preparing a longer and more thorough paper on Guerrier and her enterprising activities in Boston's North End. The opportunity came with a sabbatical leave in 1985, during which the university allowed me to investigate the career of Edith Guerrier with the objective of publishing a tidy, article-length study.

My search for documentation eventually took me to the Old Dartmouth Historical Society in New Bedford, the home of Edith Guerrier's mother's family, the Ricketsons. Although I hoped to find something of value there, I was not prepared for the astonishing collection that presented itself: a large archive that included Ricketson family papers in wonderful variety, letters, photographs, diaries, and, most welcome of all, a complete autobiography written by Edith Guerrier herself. She had started writing it in 1950 at the age of eighty, adding as a final coda, a note about the fifty-first anniversary celebration of the Saturday Evening Girls.

My thoughts of an article-length study instantly vanished, to be replaced by a desire to edit the autobiography, which I believe she had clearly intended to publish, and see it into print.

Although I have added no extraneous material or in any way rearranged the order of her manuscript, I have made excisions. I have omitted her discursively genealogical "Part I" on the history of her forebears, while making liberal use of the material in my own introduction, and considerably compressed the last several chapters of the autobiography that describe her life from the time she went to Washington to serve in Herbert Hoover's Food Administration in 1917.

Since the account she left of the period from 1917 forward is so much less spirited and engaging than the account of her earlier years, I have pruned it of those portions that lack any particular historical or personal interest. I suspect that she herself found her first fifty years more interesting, and worth remembering, than the later decades, a circumstance which, if true, explains the difference in substance and texture between the first and last sections of her autobiography.

Overall I have tried, in my introduction and the editing process, to be faithful to what I think was the essential Edith Guerrier. In a wish to provide an honest reflection of the values of her period, I have retained her chosen vocabulary, along with what might be interpreted as its loaded messages about her attitudes toward ethnicity and physical handicap. Therefore, I have let stand her attempts to record the shattered sounds of a child struggling with speech impairment, her references to "colored" girls, and her amused recounting of an Italian immigrant's broken English. I hasten to add, however, that she seems to have been about as free of racial and religious prejudice as anyone of her generation.

Although she grew to maturity in a period when many women were exerting every effort to assert themselves as independent human beings, she pursued a career for a very practical reason: she needed to earn her livelihood. When she called on the manager of the settlement house day nursery with a letter of introduction, she was not seeking to establish her identity: she simply wanted a job. She persevered there because she found congenial work in an environment that permitted her abilities to flourish and, one may surmise, because the environment also had a place for her cherished companion, Edith Brown. She took little part in the major feminist battle of her generation, woman's suffrage, although a biographical note in the *Woman's Who's Who of America* of 1914–1915 records that she was in favor of it, but she worked very hard to improve the lot of the young women who fell to her charge, encouraging them to continue with their education and helping them to find opportunities for employment that were superior to the factories or shops that would otherwise have claimed them. However, she worked through establishment channels.

In many ways a very conventional woman, respectful of the kind of wealth and position represented by women like Helen Storrow and men like Herbert Hoover (in part two of her autobiography [p. 197], she wrote of one such man, "Though I had never met him, I had no fear of my reception, since I knew that truly great men are simple, direct, and unaffected"), she lived a life that was much more turbulent than one would suspect from the smooth surface of her autobiography.

Guerrier always wrote very cautiously, for instance, about her relationship with her father, but their correspondence suggests that some of their encounters could not have been entirely amicable. Whatever resentment or bewilderment she felt about her childhood migrations from household to household, as her widowed father acted out his rage at her mother's family, has for the most part been discreetly suppressed.

She was even more guarded in her comments about Edith Brown, although the depth of her love and esteem is unmistakable in every word she wrote about her. Nor did she ever discuss, or even mention, her conversion to Christian Science, which surely was a major and significant decision for her, reared to adulthood in a climate of Methodism. Although Brown had joined the church in 1922, according to church membership records, Guerrier did not become a member until 3 June 1932, just three months before Brown's death from a long and painful illness. It is difficult not to draw a connection between the two events, but Guerrier did not even allude to it.

Of course, it must be remembered that Edith Guerrier was, as she titled her autobiography, "A Little Woman of New England," who would never willingly open her private life to the intrusion of strangers.

Acknowledgments

I wish to thank the Old Dartmouth Historical Society of New Bedford, Massachusetts, for permission to publish the manuscript of Guerrier's autobiography, and to add a special note of thanks to Virginia Adams, the Society's librarian, for her maintenance of an environment wonderfully conducive to productive work.

In addition, I send appreciative thanks to Jean Humez and Polly Welts Kaufman, both members of the faculty of the University of Massachusetts–Boston, for the perceptive readings they gave to the work in progress; and to Michael Winkler, the computer wizard of the university library, without whom I would have been unable to transfer the following pages from thought to print.

Finally, my gratitude goes to Barbara Kramer, the daughter of a Saturday Evening Girl, and her husband, Bernard Kramer, a professor of psychology at the university, who first introduced me to Edith Guerrier and the Saturday Evening Girls. Their sharing of information and firsthand knowledge of Guerrier and the SEG have contributed considerably to this work.

Molly Matson

 During the second quarter of the nineteenth century, Boston began to witness the arrival of large numbers of immigrants very unlike the mostly English, mostly Protestant resident population. They continued to arrive for the remainder of the nineteenth century and well into the twentieth; one demographer of the period, Frederick Bushee, called them "The Invading Host," a description that would seem to be compounded of equal parts of fear, distrust, and distaste.

Fortunately, by the end of the century a network of philanthropists and philanthropic agencies had been developed to help the strangers cope with their alien environment and to help inculcate in them the dominant American culture. Many of the primary agencies in this effort were settlement houses, a phenomenon imported from England where they had been established to provide educational advantage to English working men. In the United States they were reshaped to serve local goals of Americanizing a diverse population from a variety of ethnic stocks.

One of the women who became a part of this process was a librarian named Edith Guerrier (1870–1958), whose life ran in close tandem with the American social history of her generation. The granddaughter of an active abolitionist, she was the daughter of an English immigrant who served as a Lieutenant of Colored Infantry in the Civil War. She lived part of her girlhood in the territory of Kansas during the decades of the country's westward expansion, adventitiously became involved in settlement house work, and through that experience, in libraries, helped to found a pottery that now holds a secure place in the history of the Arts and Crafts movement, and served in Herbert Hoover's National Food Administration during the First World War. Approaching fifty by the end of the war, she continued to be actively involved in the library profession until she retired at the age of seventy, but she was no longer, as she had been during her first fifty years, at the cutting edge of the generation.

In 1950, one hundred comfortably middle-aged, middle-class women, alumnae of a settlement house club called the Saturday Evening Girls, gathered in Boston to commemorate the fifty-first anniversary of the founding of their group. All of them had been immigrants, or children of immigrants, and most of them had spent their childhoods in the crowded and unhygienic tenements of Boston's North End. Their guest of honor was the group's founder, Edith Guerrier, who was celebrating the eightieth anniversary of her birth.

Edith Guerrier was a descendant of Myles Standish and had first come to the North End in 1892 with a letter of introduction from William Lloyd Garrison II, a friend of her father's, to work in one of Pauline Agassiz Shaw's nursery schools.[1] At that time, she was as poor herself as any immigrant child. After several years she was asked to take up the task of organizing young girls into clubs, her only instructions being "to teach them worthwhile things and keep them off the streets." Later, when she became custodian of the settlement house reading room, she used this experience in managing girls' clubs to start social clubs among the room's young patrons. One of these clubs was called the Saturday Evening Girls.

The North End, to which Guerrier came in 1892, is a district of Boston that has been washed over by successive waves of immigrants since the arrival of the first settlers in the early seventeenth century. Originally Yankee territory, it was also home for Boston's first black community, more than a thousand slaves and freedmen who lived in "New Guinea" at the foot of Copp's Hill. Copp's Hill is also the site of the cemetery, established in 1659, that holds the remains of colonists with names like Mather, Hutchinson, and Eliot, as well as the bones of their black neighbors. The first Irish began to arrive sometime after 1824; by 1855, 14,000 of the 26,000 residents of the North End had been born in Ireland. Its housing stock had deteriorated badly by this time, and the area had become one of the city's most dilapidated tenement house districts. By 1895, the population included 6,800 Irish, 1,200 British, and 800 Portuguese, but also 6,200 Jews, primarily from Russia and eastern Europe, and 7,700 Italians.[2] The Irish presence then began to evaporate, but the Italian community continued to grow and eventually became the dominant ethnic presence in the North End.

Settlement house workers struggled to understand the character of the ethnic populations filling the old housing of the inner cities. Associates of Boston's South End House, under the editorship of their director, Robert A. Woods, published several studies on the subject, their analyses often revealing as much about them as about their clientele.

One South End House associate, Frederick A. Bushee, who wrote on demography, explained the Jewish presence in the North End by saying that Jews had emigrated from Russia because of long conflict between Jew and Gentile, the Gentiles having organized riots against the Jews who had "undermined" them by their "subtle Jewish methods." The czar's repressive actions against them in 1882, he said, were not "as is often supposed, the outcome of mere meaningless hatred. The case of the Russian is summed up simply in the old story of the money lending Jew." (It must be remembered that this was the era of the Immigration Restriction League, which at its inception in 1894 was concerned only with the exclusion of "undesirable" immigrants, but soon developed strong racial and religious biases. One of its members was Robert A. Woods.) However, Bushee went on, Jewish children were among the brightest in the schools and, when they could afford it, went on to high school and even college.[3]

He looked more favorably on the North End Italians. He described them as peasants who had come to America to escape the poverty of southern Italy, and he thought them the most illiterate of any western European immigrants (with the exception of the Spanish and Portuguese), unable to read and write even in Italian. The Irish in the North End, on the other hand, were not recent immigrants, but belonged in the main to the class of the "permanently poor" and did not welcome the influx of Jews and Italians, often subjecting them to various kinds of petty persecution. However, he noted, Italians and Jews got along more compatibly with each other than either group did with the Irish. By 1900, the North End had 28,000 residents, 80 percent of whom were Jewish, Italian, or Irish.[4]

The same year Bushee was writing, 1903, another South End associate, Edward C. Chandler, wrote that Ward 6 (the North End) had more deaths from pneumonia, meningitis, typhoid fever, and diphtheria than any other ward in Boston, and had the second highest number of deaths from cholera infantum and bronchitis (it also led in homicides). Even though many of its worst buildings had been razed on the orders of the Board of Health, under authority granted it by the state legislature in 1897, many of those left were equally unfit. Chandler held that "the personal habits of the tenants are largely responsible for such conditions. . . . Undoubtedly many a suitable tenement house is turned into a place of misery by the ignorance and vice of its occupants."[5]

Despite the uncharitable, but unfortunately rather representative judgments cited above, social reformers, philanthropists, and young people looking for a meaningful calling flocked to the North End: Pauline Agassiz Shaw, Helen Osborne Storrow, women volunteers from the Associated Charities, and the Edith Guerriers of the working world came to provide social services, various kinds of vocational instruction—and often the money to pay for them—and role models.

In 1879 a group of women volunteers had established the North End Industrial Home as a settlement house to provide classes in sewing and laundry. The next year they asked Pauline Shaw to fund a day nursery in their building so that they could offer mothers in domestic service a place to leave their children while they went to work. Forthcoming was not only a day nursery for children from eighteen months of age to three years, but a kindergarten for those from three to six. The managers also requested a circulating library and reading room, both of which, underwritten by the parish of King's Chapel, were open to women and children in the afternoon and to men in the evening.[6]

The public schools, whose population was 90 percent Jewish or Italian, also offered evening classes, attended primarily by Jews and Italians who came to learn English. In addition the North Bennet Street Industrial School (originally the North End Industrial Home) and the North End Union supplemented the grammar school curriculum with free classes and social clubs. The Industrial School taught manual training, carpentry, printing, and leather work for boys, and sewing and cooking for girls.

The social clubs were intended not only to spur Americanization but also to provide an antidote for the conflict of disparate ethnic and national elements in the North End. Most of the clubs catered to only one nationality: members of the Wiltsie Literary Club, which met to study music, literature, and Jewish history, were all Jewish girls; the

"Lilies of the Arno" were Italian girls; and the Clover Club, Irish girls. The school would have liked to integrate them, but the girls in the main preferred separate organizations, although Edith Guerrier's Saturday Evening Girls, which was the most successful club of all, attracted both Jewish and Italian girls. There were also clubs for boys that were credited with improving the boys' "social habits and attitudes," such as reducing their addiction to smoking and swearing.[7]

Although settlement houses and public libraries invariably encouraged reading to stimulate the Americanization process, they were sometimes quite cynical about the possibilities of such activity achieving success. Boston Public Library's *Annual Report* for 1898 (No. 46) noted that although the library had been delivering books twice weekly to the Hancock Grammar School for Girls in the North End, it considered the area "as unpromising a field as could be chosen for this experiment, the children being largely of foreign birth or parentage." Despite this reservation, however, the delivery station was well patronized and by 1899 had had to be discontinued because the circulation—7,000 volumes for the school year 1898–99—had begun to overtax the teacher in charge. The delivery station was transferred to the North Bennet Street Industrial School and in November 1899 became a regular station of the Boston Public Library with daily book delivery and Edith Guerrier as custodian.

Settlement houses and libraries also played another role: They provided opportunities for useful employment, sometimes gainful, sometimes not, to educated, middle-class, single women who were beginning to look for rewarding work outside their homes. Most of these women came from old American families, many from well-to-do families, important because settlement house work was usually unpaid. Libraries valued them, in addition to their other qualities, because they were content with small salaries. As early as 1877 the director of Boston Public Library, Justin Winsor, had already recognized that fact, saying that women "for the money they cost . . . are infinitely better than equivalent salaries will produce of the other sex." Libraries, he added, could have their pick of educated young women;[8] they continued to have their pick until the 1920s.

When Guerrier stood at the door of Pauline Shaw's nursery school in the North End in 1892, she shared most of the characteristics of other settlement house staff, although she had only a seminary, not a college, degree, and she was not well-to-do at all, save in memory. She had had, moreover, a rather less conventional past than most of her peers, having survived the loss of her mother when she was three and an unsettled childhood, shuttling back and forth between the securely upper-middle-class, well-provisioned household of her maternal grandparents, where no one worked for a living, and the bare-bones frugality of her paternal uncle's Methodist parsonage.

Her mother's family, the Ricketsons, were prominent citizens of New Bedford. Her grandfather, Daniel Ricketson, had retired in 1841 at the age of twenty-eight when his father died and left him "a sufficient competence to provide a home for his family, without engaging in a business or professional career, for which he had neither inclination nor aptitude."[9] He did, however, incline to letter writing and frequently wrote to literary figures, such as Emerson, Whittier, and Thoreau, whose work he admired. Many of these eminent men surprisingly enough wrote back, and Mr. Ricketson accumulated large packets of letters and often established personal relationships with his correspondents. Of his four children, two, Anna and Walton, never married, but shared their lives and their household until Walton died in 1923, and as often as possible served as treasured surrogate parents for their beloved niece Edith.

Her paternal grandfather was named Samuel Guerrier, according to a report written by her father, and "was of Huguenot descent, one of a body settling on the banks of the Thames about 1685." Her great-grandfather, George Guerrier, was a farmer on the Isle of Dogs,[10] and when he died he left considerable property, but Samuel Guerrier's portion of the inheritance was swallowed up in an unsuccessful book-publishing enterprise. "He subsequently pursued clerical occupations, having but a precarious subsistence thro' many years, & finally died in the care of my halfbrother Will G. at an advanced age."[11]

Her father, another George Guerrier, was born in England in 1837, and had been a freight clerk before emigrating to America in 1856. Sometime before 1860 he had shared a short-lived business venture with Joseph Ricketson of New Bedford, Daniel Ricketson's younger brother, but by 1861 he had been mustered into the 22nd Massachusetts Volunteers as a private soldier, taking part by his own account "in the peninsular campaign under General McClellan, in the assaults upon and the siege of Yorktown, the battles of Hanover Court House, Mechanicsville, and Gaines' Mill." He was slightly wounded at Gaines' Mill, taken prisoner, and held at Richmond for almost two months until returned in a prisoner exchange. On 29 May 1863, he was appointed a Second Lieutenant of Colored Infantry and attached to the 35th Regiment, U.S. Colored Troops. He participated "in the siege and occupation of Fort Wagner, the demonstration upon Charleston, S.C. of the autumn and winter of 1863; in the battle of Olustee, Fla, Feb. 20th 1864; and in numerous skirmishes and marches."[12] In June of 1864 he was granted a medical certificate on the grounds that he was "subject to severe neuralgic attacks of the head brought on by exposure to excessive heat of the sun," and permitted to resign from military service.[13] In the following year he apparently considered reenlisting, but Joseph Ricketson, in a letter from Boston dated 19 May 1865, advised against it, remarking that one with a "decent situation" (with the Chicago, Burlington, and Quincy Railroad) should keep it.[14]

On 2 September 1867, George Guerrier married Daniel Ricketson's younger daughter Emma while her father was away from home. According to Edith Guerrier, the young couple had been encouraged to marry by Emma's mother, Louisa, but had not secured the approval of the bride's father, an omission that may have partially accounted for later events related to Emma's inheritance. Performing the ceremony was George Guerrier's uncle, chaplain of New Bedford's Seamen's Bethel, the Methodist minister Samuel Fox.

Three years later Edith was born, and shortly thereafter Guerrier's employment took him west. He left his wife and daughter in New Bedford waiting for the summons to join him. His wife wrote him frequently and, in a letter dated 12 September 1871 addressed to Garden Grove, Iowa, asked about "your soldiers right to 160 acres, can't you get it somewhere in Iowa you know it would amount to something for Edith if not for ourselves."[15] (A receipt dated 22 February 1872 indicates that Guerrier did acquire land under the Homestead Act, but on the back is a note reading "160 acres of excellent land at Inland, Neb: forfeited by non-residence owing to Emma's sickness.")[16]

By 28 April 1872 she was looking forward to their reunion. "I think of you dear George in that little house all alone, soon the patter of little feet will gladden it for you." Her last line, added in a postscript, was, "Shall I leave packing till your arrival?"[17] but she was dead of consumption before the removal west could take place. The financial settlement, which Guerrier had always assumed his father-in-law would provide as a marriage portion (as he had provided for Emma's brother Arthur), had never been made, and he became obsessed with the feeling that he had been ill-used.

After his wife's death he removed his daughter from the care of her mother's family in New Bedford and deposited her in the parsonage of his uncle Samuel Fox in East Thompson, Connecticut. This was not the first time his uncle had been on hand at a crucial moment in his life. It seems safe to surmise, for instance, that Guerrier had been walking on the Acushnet Road in 1862, where he reputedly first met his future father-in-law Daniel Ricketson, because his uncle was then resident in the town of Acushnet, and it was, of course, Uncle Fox who was summoned to perform the ceremony when Guerrier and Emma Ricketson impetuously decided to marry. Now the old minister was called upon to provide a home for his widowed nephew's daughter.

At the time Edith came to live in his household in 1874, Fox was a patriarchal sixty-one, but he continued in active ministry, interspersed with short periods of superannuation, until 1890. He had come to America in 1833 at the age of twenty, made one voyage on a New Bedford whaler, worked briefly for a New Bedford merchant, experienced a religious conversion, and resigned to enter the Methodist itinerancy. During his ministerial career he held appointments in a total of nineteen pulpits in Massachusetts, Connecticut, and Rhode Island, most of them for only one- or two-year periods, in accordance with Methodist practice.[18] His longest tenure was the period of 1863 to 1869 when he was chaplain of the Seamen's Bethel of the New Bedford Port Society, the chapel where the crew of the *Pequod* was blessed before their departure for the South Seas in *Moby Dick*.

When he died in 1903, an editorial in the *New Bedford Evening Standard* described him as the last survivor in that region of the old type of circuit-riding Methodist preacher who went "from the shop straight into the pulpit." He "heard the call, and never doubting, began to preach the Gospel, with no other preparation than his boyhood schooling, his one voyage on a whaler, his short experience in business, and his belief in God and in his mission."[19]

Edith spent three periods of her childhood living with Uncle Fox and his family in parsonages in East Thompson, in Mapleville, Rhode Island, and Pocasset on Cape Cod. In between East Thompson and Mapleville she returned to her mother's sister and brother, Aunt Anna and Uncle Walton, in New Bedford; between Mapleville and Pocasset she stayed with her father in Concord, where his stiff-necked sister

Margaret had come to manage his household, and after Aunt Margaret (much to Edith's relief) returned to England, in the Boston suburb of Brookline. While she was in Pocasset her father received a transfer to Burlington, Iowa, and with little preamble snatched thirteen-year-old Edith from her Pocasset schoolroom to travel west with him. In the fall he enrolled her in boarding school in Burlington and went to see his brother Sam in Atchison, Kansas. By the end of her spring term (in 1885), Guerrier was managing a lumberyard his brother had recently opened in Kendall, a prairie town in western Kansas. He moved Edith from Burlington to Sam Guerrier's house in Atchison, where she remained while he went back to Kendall to build a house for her. The next year he judged that Edith, now almost sixteen, was old enough to keep house for him and brought her to live on the prairie, but he kept her with him for only a year.

During the summer of 1887 he decided to send her back East to school, and in the fall she entered the Vermont Methodist Seminary and Female College in Montpelier. She heard frequently from her father in letters filled with discussions of literature—"I knew you would like Ruskin when you once took hold. I have been an omnivorous reader myself, & should know how to discriminate—with the sense that my heart is right, at least, if I have not also some critical faculty"[20]—and laced with furious reproaches of the Ricketsons: "I feel the necessity of watching them closely, they are so sinister and tricky," adding that he wanted her to be on her guard, "for it is in the cruel and wicked hearts of these folks to excite prejudice against me, which they did in Concord, New Bedford & Boston, & I was glad to get away from it all."[21]

After four years she remembered as the "pleasantest" of her life, she graduated on 25 June 1891, one of a class of seventeen. She had won second honors and at the graduation exercises read her poem, "The Great American Desert." In the school history published in 1962 she is listed as one of the "graduates who went on to achieve distinction in later life."[22] Upon graduating she first thought of becoming a professional artist and, with her father's encouragement, enrolled in the Museum School of Boston's Museum of Fine Arts.

Her father meanwhile never ceased fulminating against the Ricketsons, still convinced that they owed him money. He wrote Edith that she should respond to a check received from her Aunt Anna by asking: "Who is to turn over to me my mother's marriage portion of two thousand dolls., with the interest, which papa tells me has never been paid, and which belongs rightfully to me for my benefit? My idea was the money you have been writing of bore some relation to the amount."[23] A month later he expanded on this theme: "Of course, in taking money, your attitude is clear that you receive it as your right, and that—it is needless for you to make any explanations to the R's of the ground you take it on."[24] There is no indication that Edith took his advice.

Despite the occasional check from the Ricketsons, she found she needed additional income to survive. A fellow student suggested that she apply for a job in one of Pauline Shaw's nursery schools, and her application was accepted. For a time, although she withdrew from the Museum School in favor of a free evening class, she continued studying art, but never took a degree. In the course of her work in the museum, however, she met another student, a "pretty young thing, shy as a fawn, [who] stood day after day with her eyes fixed on her work. Apparently no one spoke to her and apparently she spoke to no one. . . . One day, in passing her easel, I spoke to her. She replied without raising her eyes. Every day after that first time, I spoke, and before long Edith Brown and I began taking walks together on Sunday afternoons." Edith Brown quickly became one of the most significant figures in her life, her closest friend and colleague, with whom she shared her professional and domestic life for forty years, until Brown's death.

After several years in North Bennet Street, Guerrier was asked to exchange her duties in the nursery for the task of taking charge of five girls' clubs, then being organized in local neighborhood houses, and of maintaining the girls' reading room at North Bennet Street. In 1899 the girls' and the boys' reading rooms at North Bennet became a regular station of the Boston Public Library with Edith Guerrier as custodian.[25]

She started story-hour groups for girls of various ages, the youngest group consisting of fourth graders and the oldest, who met on Saturday evening, high-school girls. These groups caught the interest of Helen Osborne Storrow, a member of the Board of Managers of the North Bennet Street Industrial School and the philanthropic wife of the wealthy Boston lawyer and civic leader, James Jackson Storrow. Especially interested in the Saturday Evening Girls, as they were called, she continued her support as they moved from high school into the working world, funding many of their activities, including summer vacations at a rented farm in the Plymouth Woods and then at a camp at Wingaersheek Beach in West Gloucester, which she purchased.

In 1906 Guerrier, using money inherited from her grandfather, Daniel Ricketson, began building a house in the Chestnut Hill section of Boston for herself and Brown and her father. Her father, however, was beginning to grow old and troubled. Her uncle Walton, in a diary entry dated 14 March 1906, commented that his niece and her father had come to dinner, "Edith looking very well and happy over the prospect of a home of her own, for herself and her father, Geo seems somewhat aged and rather 'losing ground,' as we say, to put it gently."[26]

Guerrier was indeed losing ground, and his daughter was beginning to lose patience with him. From Lincoln, where she and Edith Brown were spending the summer in the house of the philanthropic Helen Storrow (while the latter was in Europe), she wrote, "Perhaps you better keep this letter so you will have something to refer to when wondering when you are to be at Chestnut Hill," but she added that his coming at all "depends wholly on yourself—If you take this opportunity to show that you can still maintain control over your emotions & actions you shall be with us as soon as we can conveniently have you." Her final admonition was, "One helpful thing which I will suggest would be to try to think what you can do to please others rather than what others can do to please you. Also try to understand what it pleases others to have you do for them rather than what it pleases you to do for them whether they like it or not." It is interesting to note that this last piece of advice was also the moral of a story, "Ai and the Three Armadillos," one of six animal stories in her children's book, *Wanderfolk in Wonderland*, illustrated by Edith Brown and published in 1903. A postscript to the letter reads, "Kindly keep this & read it when you feel like asking questions."[27]

In reply to this and other similar notes, her father answered, in part, "Your letters read so cold, so cold You have not yet given me the reason for desiring me not to come to Boston Please be plain in your next—very next," and at the end, "Oh, my dear child what is all this mystery? I have done no wrong—I wanted that house and you and I in it. God pity me I am weeping!"[28] In April 1907, he was admitted to McLean Hospital, diagnosed as suffering from arteriosclerotic dementia. Helen Storrow promptly sent the two Ediths to Europe.

George Guerrier lived at McLean for four years until his death of acute lobar pneumonia in July 1911.[29] His history had painfully replicated his father's, from the will-o'-the-wisp inheritance—the marriage portion he thought due him from his wife's family—to his own "precarious subsistence" at "clerical occupations" in his later years. A man with a deep love of literature and a published poet,[30] he was aggrieved by his lack of educational advantage. "Oh how it makes me sigh to think I could not have had a college education!" he had written to his daughter in 1890. "Fancy one going out into the world (with my taste) at twelve years of age—at common drudgery, too—to earn a living."[31]

In 1908, encouraged by Helen Storrow, Guerrier and Brown began to develop a small pottery—an idea generated by the art pottery they had seen during their recent European tour—as a means of creating useful employment for the maturing young women in the Saturday Evening Girls (SEG). They found an old potter in Charlestown to teach them how to throw, after which they bought a kick wheel and a small kiln, then located an English pottery chemist to teach them glaze formulas and the techniques of firing glazed and unglazed pottery. Their first experiments as pottery making took place in the basement of their house in Chestnut Hill and were continued, after the summer camp season was over, in West Gloucester, but the transportation problems from that site proved insurmountable.

To provide a proper home for the pottery and room for Guerrier's girls' clubs, Storrow bought a four-story brick building at 18 Hull Street in the North End to serve as the library clubhouse. Its basement and half of the first floor were converted into a small, but complete pottery, which was christened the Paul Revere Pottery since it stood almost in the shadow of the Old North Church where the famous lantern had hung. The building also housed the activities of all Guerrier's library clubs, those from the grammar and high school as well as the older Saturday Evening Girls, and a model apartment on the top floor. The two Ediths rented their Chestnut Hill house to friends and moved into the model apartment.[32]

By 1914 Helen Storrow felt she could not continue to support both the clubs and the pottery and decided to concentrate on the latter. The clubs were allotted permanent quarters in the basement of the new North End Branch Library, which had opened in 1913, and the clubhouse was put up for sale. The proceeds were used to finance the construction of a new building especially designed for the pottery on Nottingham Hill in the Brighton section of Boston. By the end of 1915 the clubhouse had been closed and the new quarters were ready. Guerrier and Brown moved to Brighton, and the *S.E.G. News* reported, "Every S.E.G. who has believed in the possibilities of the Pottery, who has rejoiced to watch the experiment of working out a happy, paying industry, will be justified in feeling an honest pride that the new year finds . . . the Paul Revere Pottery not only situated on a hill-top, but literally founded on a rock, which is the best augury of success one could have."[33]

Not only did the pottery provide work for the newly adult members of the SEG, but it also provided a workplace dedicated to fine craftsmanship organized on enlightened principles of management. The Girls worked an eight-hour day in an airy, well-lit work environment, received a decent wage with an annual paid vacation, and a daily hot lunch. They were also encouraged to continue their education, and many of them did. Unfortunately, although the Paul Revere ware sold well, the pottery never became financially independent, but instead required considerable and constant subsidy to stay alive.

Guerrier, of course, continued to be the librarian of the North End Branch, but in 1917, as a volunteer for the War Service Committee of the Women's City Club, she made a trip to Washington to gather material on food conservation for the Boston Food Facts Bureau. She was almost immediately asked to return to be chief of the library section of Herbert Hoover's National Food Administration. She accepted, thinking her stint there would be short, but she stayed in the capital until 1919, eventually writing a book about her experience, *We Pledged Allegiance, a Librarian's Intimate Story of the United States Food Administration*. Published in 1941 by the Stanford University Press in this country and the Oxford University Press in England, it was the first title of the Hoover Library series of Miscellaneous Publications on War, Revolution, and Peace.

When she resettled in Boston she found herself assigned to the main library of Boston Public with the title of "Supervisor of Circulation," her old post in the North End having been filled. In 1922 she and Brown again visited Europe and, on their return, learned that during her absence Guerrier had become the supervisor of branch libraries, a post she held for the next eighteen years. But the years brought changes. Her uncle Walton died in 1923 and her beloved aunt Anna in 1929. In 1932 Edith Brown died.

An obituary in the *Boston Transcript*, written by Guerrier, commended her old friend as "a master craftsman known . . . as one of the outstanding American potters," adding that at the Paul Revere Pottery, of which she was a founder, "many young girls became potters under the guidance of their director, who taught them not only how to mold the plastic clay but by the nobility of her character inspired them to mold their lives after a higher and more spiritual pattern."[34] Born in Nova Scotia in 1872, Edith Brown had come to Boston to attend the Museum School, from which she graduated in 1895, then stayed on to work as a teacher of drawing and design. She also developed some small reputation as an illustrator, her first published drawings appearing in a periodical called *The Churchman* in 1899, and later in children's books. In 1907 she became interested in pottery and was chiefly responsible for the development of the Paul Revere Pottery, serving as its director, as well as the director of the school of ceramics that grew up around it, until she died. The pottery, which had been operating at ever-increasing losses for many years, finally closed its doors in 1942.

In 1940, at the age of seventy, Guerrier fell victim to mandatory retirement. When her friends congratulated her on the leisure she would now have to do the things she had always wanted to do, she retorted that the activities in which she had engaged for most of her life *were* the things she always wanted to do. Her adult life had been filled with purposeful activity and she wanted to continue it. She also lamented that the retirement she had always looked forward to sharing with the other Edith would now have to be faced alone.

World War II, however, provided new opportunity for useful work. Although she was initially rejected by five service organizations, who thought her too old to be of assistance, she persisted until she found a congenial post as the full-time unpaid volunteer librarian of the Massachusetts Committee on Public Safety, collecting and disseminating information on dealing with potential disasters, such as bombs, and on preparing for blackouts and possible evacuation. In 1945, when the war ended, her library files became archives and she was once again, and this time permanently, out of a job.

Edith Guerrier died in 1958, leaving her estate to the Christian Science Church, after the payment of lifetime trusts for two old companions. She was eighty-eight years old.

A resilient and independent child, Guerrier developed into a strong, self-reliant, productive adult despite the unsettled circumstances of her childhood. She had some assistance along the way. For much of her adult life she had had the close emotional support of a secure relationship with a valued and compatible life companion, and from her early twenties the emotional and financial support of her mother's family. Finally, she had been able at crucial times to draw assistance, especially access to powerful patrons, from the network of her family's connections with influential Bostonians.

The most important of these was Helen Osborne Storrow. It is clear that a good portion of Guerrier's work with the young women of the North End would have been impossible without the generosity of Helen Storrow, whose uncle was George Guerrier's friend, William Lloyd Garrison II. George Guerrier and Garrison had much in common: both had been enthusiastic abolitionists, both advocated equal rights for women, and both wrote poetry, on which they often exchanged comments. Garrison also came to Guerrier's assistance in time of need; many of the latter's letters to his daughter in 1891 and 1892 are on the business stationery of his employer, the Edison Electric Illuminating Company, which lists W. L. Garrison as treasurer.

Garrison's wife, Ellen, was a daughter of Martha Coffin Wright and a niece of Lucretia Coffin Mott, both celebrated members of the women's rights movement. A poem of Garrison's entitled "Human Equality,"[35] sent to George Guerrier for critical comment, is a ringing defense of women's rights. The marriage of Ellen Osborne and W. L. Garrison II, son of the famous abolitionist, had united two families that shared compatible interests.

In 1891 their niece Helen married James Jackson Storrow, Jr., a Harvard-educated lawyer, partner in the Boston law firm of Fish, Richardson, and Storrow, and the newlyweds set up housekeeping on Beacon Street. In 1900 James Storrow gave up law to become a senior partner in the banking firm of Lee, Higginson, & Company, and the Storrows rather quickly became rich. Helen Storrow began to develop extensive philanthropic interests. She became a member of the board of the North Bennet Street Industrial School, contributed generously to the Saturday Evening Girls, underwrote many activities for the Girl Scouts (the organization that was probably the major and most absorbing effort of her lifetime), and offered substantive support to many other social and cultural enterprises.[36]

If it was a letter from Storrow's uncle W. L. Garrison II that provided Edith Guerrier's original entrée to the nursery school at North Bennet Street, it was Storrow's capital that provided the Saturday Evening Girls with a summer camp in West Gloucester, a library clubhouse on Hull Street, and a pottery workshop in Brighton. It was Edith Guerrier, however, who carried all these ventures to success.

❧ In 1954 Guerrier collected the reminiscences of forty living members of the Saturday Evening Girls in a supplement (the "Cherry Tree Edition") to the *S.E.G. News*, the library clubhouse newspaper published by the Girls from 1912 to 1917. She asked each of them to conclude with a few words on what America meant to her. The answers were predictable.

"Freedom."

"Opportunity."

"Home."

The successful assimilation of these women into the middle-class mainstream, however, was somewhat less predictable. At least a portion of the credit for their progress from tenement to suburbia belongs to the few men and the many women—like Edith Guerrier—who bent their best efforts to improve the language, modify the behavior, and inculcate traditional New England values into the minds of the immigrants and children of immigrants who sought out the settlement houses and night schools and libraries that offered them a chance at full membership in American society.

The SEG, an outstanding example of this endeavor, was the outcome of the Saturday evening story hour of the North Bennet Street Library, where Edith Guerrier was the custodian. Girls who patronized the library were invited to attend half hour talks on Saturday evenings on topics like literature, art, music, social problems, and economic questions. It was noted that the same girls tended to appear for each lecture, and in a matter of time they inevitably formed a club. They read and discussed what they read, held dancing parties, went to the theater, visited historic places, gave concerts, and presented plays.[37] In the spring of 1906 they gave a "careful performance" of *A Midsummer Night's Dream*, in 1907 an "unusual performance" of *The Merchant of Venice*, which they repeated out-of-doors in Lincoln, Massachusetts, on Memorial Day for friends of the North Bennet Street Industrial School, and in 1909 an "excellent presentation" of *Hamlet*. Their glee club sang a cantata, Carl Reinecke's "Snowdrop."[38]

It is not surprising that twenty-seven of the thirty-six contributors to the Cherry Tree Edition (all told, there were forty contributors, but four of the respondents did not indicate their educational status) had attended high school, even though high school was not such a given in pre–World War I America. Eight had attended college or normal school, and one, the New England Conservatory of Music. In 1910 only 3.8

percent of eighteen- to twenty-one-year-old women in the United States were in college, a figure that rose only to 7.6 percent in 1920,[39] but 25 percent of the Saturday Evening Girls in this sample attended college or professional schools. Of the forty-eight children of alumnae whose mothers had provided educational data, forty attended college, ten going to Harvard or Radcliffe and the rest to institutions from Bates College in Maine to the University of California at Berkeley.

As the mentor of this group of women whose lives she had worked to mold—as they had once worked to mold Paul Revere plates and bowls—Guerrier carefully considered her answer to the citizenship question she had posed them. She wrote, "BEING AN AMERICAN means that it is my duty to understand the Government of my country and to do my part as a conscientious citizen by using my voting privilege righteously, humbly seeking wisdom from God to direct me."[40] It is in some ways a curious statement, limiting her identity as a citizen to an intelligent exercise of her voting franchise, coupled with a reverent nod to her deity. The subtext is more abundant. It speaks to her commitment to education, to democratic ideals of citizen participation coupled with service to one's community, and—perhaps a slight resonance from her Methodist girlhood—to a belief in the guiding hand of an omniscient parent.

AN
INDEPENDENT
WOMAN

Edith Guerrier as a young girl. Reproduced courtesy of the Whaling Museum, New Bedford, Massachusetts.

A Motherless Child,
1870–1883

 It is good to be alive! That is how I feel today, and that is how I felt seventy-seven years ago when, at the age of three, I ran away, taking as baggage my toothbrush. I had a great longing to escape from the kind but timid grandparents, aunts, and uncles who helped my mother bring me up. Beyond the stone posts that marked our driveway lay a white road, which I was sure led to the end of the rainbow in Fairyland; that was where I was going, and that was where I was found by a good Quaker in a broad-brimmed hat.

I tried to make him understand that I was in Fairyland and that I was going to live in the lovely meadow with the pretty violets and the pink apple blossoms, and he tried to make me understand that good little girls did not run away from their grandmas and grandpas, their mothers and fathers, and their aunts and uncles. The upshot of the matter was that the good Quaker took me right out of Fairyland and drove me home in his little gig, drawn by a big white horse with the biggest pink hoofs I had ever seen.

This was my first great adventure. I thought it out by myself, I carried it out by myself, and it was better than I had dreamed it could be. The fact that at the age of three I had found the end of the rainbow to be a field of flowers gave me an assurance, which has never left me, of the happy end of all adventure.

I was duly wept over by my womenfolk, who each in turn tried to impress upon me the enormity of my crime against society, as represented by my family.

"What should I have done if the fairies had kept my little Edie?" sobbed my mother.

"Picked another little Edie," shouted the unmoved cause of this grief, who knew that she had been found in the garden neatly wrapped in a cabbage leaf.

When I was three and a half, my mother died. I have been told again and again that she was a very beautiful woman, possessed of an unusually fine mind. To this was added the postscript, "You do not resemble her in any way." Yet the faint memories of those far-distant days at Brooklawn, near New Bedford, Massachusetts, have little in them of my beautiful mother. I seem to have been always the center of the picture, a merry, carefree child in *my* house and *my* garden surrounded by grown folks who usually did what I wanted them to do. If, however, they displeased me, I disciplined them by making myself cry.

After my mother's death, my father decided to take me away from my retinue of devoted relatives and from the fine old mansion in the midst of orchards and gardens, where I had spent the first three years of a happy childhood. I was bewildered, not knowing whether to laugh or to cry. I had on my frilled bonnet and best light blue coat, and was going with Papa on the choo-choo to see Aunty Fox. This was something to be glad about, but where was Mama, and why were all the grown folks crying, even Grandpa and the grown-up uncles? Not knowing what to do, I did nothing, but allowed myself to be kissed and cried over, then I trotted away, holding fast to my father's finger.

Now Aunty Fox lived in the Methodist parsonage in East Thompson, Connecticut, with Uncle Fox and four young Foxes. To break the journey, which was a long one for a little child, we stayed overnight at Aunt Fanny's in Boston;[1] and my father has often told me that one of the most difficult tasks he ever undertook was getting my clothes off at night and getting them on in the morning, a feat he insisted on performing, for his training and for mine. Sad as he was, he laughed till the tears ran down his face when I escaped with nothing on, and he could not catch me, as there was nothing to get hold of.

In due course we arrived at the plain little parsonage surrounded by a neat, white picket fence. As we opened the gate, Aunty Fox came to the door, her face wreathed in smiles. She sat down on the doorstep and held out her arms. I felt the generous love that welcomed me, and stretching out my own arms ran into her embrace.

I was not in the least disturbed when my father left the next morning. It had always been like that at Brooklawn, my real home. Every Monday morning, while it was still dark, Papa had gone off to Boston; and every

Saturday night, just after I had been bathed and put in my little bed, he came home. I could have told you that he worked all the week in a place called "office" to make Sunday, that he came home Saturday night to bring it to us, and that when it was over he went back to make another one.

At East Thompson I was surprised that we had Sunday without him. I was sure that he had nothing to do with the kind of Sundays we had there, which were called "Sabbaths." On the first one, at our very early breakfast, Uncle Fox made snarling noises because his toast was burned. He seemed to feel that Aunty had burned it purposely to annoy him. Poor Aunty began to cry, and at that he growled, "Don't be a baby; eat your breakfast."

Fourteen-year-old Lizzie and twelve-year-old Susie looked at their mother pityingly, but said never a word. As for me, I beat the table with my spoon and shouted, "Naughty, naughty man to make poor Aunty cry." At that Aunty stopped crying instantly and said, "Little Edie must be a good girl, and good little girls are seen and not heard."

The utter lack of logic in Aunty's behavior impressed me, baby as I was. For the first time I felt resentment, not against poor Aunty but against naughty Uncle Fox, and when later on in the day I heard Uncle thundering from the pulpit, shaking his long white locks, and wagging his patriarchal beard, I sensed that his God was the kind that would yell at anyone who burned toast or scorched a linen collar or laughed in church. I could not realize then that Uncle Fox had to support his family on the meager salary of three hundred dollars a year. I did not know that because of gratitude to God for saving his life in an extraordinary manner, he had vowed to preach the power of His Word as long as he lived. I did not know that burned toast and scorched collars meant a money loss, and that even a tenth of a penny had to be considered. In short, it was to be years and years before I would learn to judge according to "the evidence of things not seen."

On that first Sabbath I sat with the minister's daughters, Susie and Lizzie, in the singers' gallery at the back of the church, directly opposite the pulpit. Lizzie played the melodeon with great spirit and sang lustily. Susie sang with equal vigor. I suppose there were other singers there, but I cannot remember them.

The church with its arched windows, its high-backed pews with fat red cushions, and its long aisles carpeted with strips of crimson drugget, was the most magnificent building I had ever seen. I was so awed that I tried my best to behave like a grown-up. Grown-ups sat very straight; grown-ups looked cross when they wished to be impressive; grown-ups—and then a dreadful thing happened, so dreadful a thing that looking back across the years I tremble as I think of it—I fell asleep in the midst of the preaching. How long I slept I do not know, but I was wakened suddenly by a fierce beating of rain on the gallery windows. Before I was sufficiently awake to know where I was, I cried out, "Look, Lizzie, it's raining." Instantly I knew what I had done, and the fear of some mysterious punishment was so intense that the incident is indelibly etched in my memory.

After church came Sunday school, where each child was given a little brightly colored picture of some incident in Bible history. After Sunday school, we went home to dinner. Then came a long, long, long afternoon. I was not allowed to go out-of-doors, or to play indoors. Lizzie and Susie were very kind and read the Bible, and over and over again told me the story of my colored picture; but it seemed like a whole year of time from dinner until six o'clock, when we each had a bowl of crackers and milk before going to evening service. Fear kept me awake until the benediction was pronounced, when I fell asleep on my feet. Then, with Susie grasping one of my arms and Lizzie the other, I stumbled home. The only prayer I could be roused to say was, "Thank you, thank you, Sabbath is over."

I lived with Uncle and Aunty Fox, and with Lizzie and Susie, until I was a big girl of six. Sometimes I thought of Brooklawn, and of Fairyland, and once when I saw at the gate a red-and-yellow tin-peddler's cart, with a door in the back that opened upon a room filled with jingling pans and dippers, I knew that it had come from Fairyland. Watching for my chance, when Uncle Fox, surrounded by his womenfolk, had gone into the house proudly bearing one small utensil, I managed to elude my elders and was off and away, trailing the jingling cart over the brow of the hill. Just as I was explaining to the peddler that I wanted to ride with him, that I was always a good girl, and could dress myself, and button my boots, Lizzie arrived in breathless haste. With no word to the peddler, she grabbed my hand and began to run down the hill, dragging me so fast that my feet fairly twinkled.

Uncle Fox, having already pronounced judgment, met me with a large flat slipper in his hand, and for the first and only time in my life, I was spanked. The next time my father came I told him how much I liked the tin peddler and his house on wheels, and how much I did not like to be spanked. I am of the opinion that he did not like it either, for it never happened again.

For some weeks I grieved that I could not know the peddler as I knew Mr. Lord, the engine driver, who drove his puffing engine along the railroad tracks directly behind the parsonage. Mr. Lord had a soul that scorned petty conventionalities. He never seemed conscious of the smudges on his face, or of the grime on his hands. The more grease he had on his overalls, the more at ease he seemed. He said he loved little children and begged Uncle Fox to let me ride with him occasionally on his engine. Shall I ever forget those glorious rides! I hope not! The creaking of the leather seat on which I sat, the hissing of the steam, the ruddy glow of the fire, and the landscape rushing past the windows of the cab were the results of my friend's magic. All he had to do was to open or shut the throttle—a beautiful word, *throttle*—and we went slowly or swiftly according to his desire.

Once when I was "half past five," I was sent by Lizzie to the village post office, which was also a general store with bolts of cotton goods on the shelves, with sugar and flour in barrels, and with potatoes and onions in baskets. Said Lizzie, "Here are six cents. You are to get five cents worth of pork, and with the other cent you may buy something for yourself."

That was the first time I had ever had a cent given me to spend. It represented to me more wealth than any money I have had since. Of course, I had always given a cent to God every Sunday, and the idea that I could have a cent just like God was very pleasing. With my cent I bought a block of jellylike substance known as jujube paste. I ate a third on the way home, and saved a bite apiece for Lizzie and Susie. Their pleasure over my generosity, as well as their enjoyment of the candy, was unfeigned. For the first time I experienced the extravagant joy of giving gifts to others. That money could buy such joy was indeed a revelation.

Now a cent's worth of jujube paste is a trifle, but poverty sat at the board in the Fox family. With his salary of three hundred dollars, Uncle Fox had brought up and educated, as education went in those days, his three sons and three daughters. At the time I became part of the household, one son and one daughter "in the churchyard lay," as the song has it, and two sons were at work in distant cities. It is small wonder that Uncle Fox suffered from an indigestion that made him querulous. The task of feeding and clothing a family on an allowance of less than a dollar a week for each person might well affect a man's digestion, as well as his disposition.

The parishioners who scraped together the three hundred dollars knew that their minister and his family were often short of provisions, and at least once a year they staged a donation party, when each member of the church brought some staple commodity to the parsonage. A favorite article was pea beans. Fortunately we were all fond of pork and beans; and Aunty Fox, who was a marvelous cook and could make even salt herring and fried mush taste as good as turkey and plum pudding, had a method of baking beans that I have never seen equalled. On one of the occasions when there was a shortage in the larder of this delightful commodity, Lizzie found me playing church. The words of my sermon are forgotten, but the words of my prayer were:

> O, Lord, we humbly pray Thee that Thou wilt remember to give us plenty of pork and beans, for which, O, Lord, we thank Thee now and forever. Amen.

The day before I was six, my father came to take me to spend my birthday with Grandpa and Grandma Ricketson in New Bedford. Aunty Fox put my meager garments into a box, clothed me in my Sunday dress, put on my little brown hat with its wreath of daisies, passed me around to be kissed by Uncle and the girls, and then stood in the doorway alternatively wiping her hands on her apron and waving them till I was out of sight.

Grandpa Ricketson no longer lived at Brooklawn. He had sold the fine old mansion, the orchards, and the lawn traversed by the brook which gave the place its name. The town house was about as plain in appearance as Uncle Fox's parsonage. It stood well back from the street and at one side was a tidy little barn in which Charley, the old white horse, and the family carryall lived.

The front yard was protected by a fence having two rails. On either side of the gateway rose two elm trees, whose green umbrellas of shade towered far above the house. A blue flagstone path ran from the gateway to the old-fashioned front "stoop," as the porch was called. This was enclosed by latticework, and on either side there were low benches. To the left was Grandmother's flower garden, where Uncle Walton saw to it that the old-fashioned flowers she loved so well provided bouquets for her room, from the "poeticas" of early spring to the button chrysanthemums of late fall. In the backyard was an old well with moss-covered bucket. During the summer it was used as a refrigerator for milk and butter. Once lowered to the surface of the water, they were kept fresh and cool.

In two-and-a-half years I had become "a big girl," but Grandpa and Grandma, Aunt Anna and Uncle Walton had not changed. It was evident that they hoped to keep me. Aunt Anna had prepared a little room, and Uncle Walton, a born craftsman, had made for it a complete set of furniture: a little bedstead, bureau, stand, and rocking chair, all of black walnut. There were white muslin curtains at the windows, and on the walls was cream-colored wallpaper covered with gold stars. On the floor was new straw matting; beside the bed was a little rug which either Grandma or Aunt Anna had knit. It was the most beautiful little room I had ever seen.

"Open the closet door," said Aunt Anna.

When I did so, I could hardly believe my eyes. There hung a perfectly new blue cashmere dress, a ruffled white pinafore with pockets, and a checked blue-and-white flannel wrapper. On the floor was a dainty pair of bedroom slippers, knit by Grandma.

"Now," said Aunt Anna, "open the bureau drawers."

Each drawer had its neat piles of handmade underclothing. There were little shirts, corded waists with rows of bone buttons, ruffled drawers, petticoats white and colored, pinafores, and stockings neatly rolled into tight balls, all new, not a patch or a darn to be seen. My heart was filled with gratitude. Once more, as in the days of my babyhood, I had around me my own people who loved me because I was their own, a kind of love unlike any other. Kneeling by my little white bed that night, I prayed aloud the usual formula, ending, "and make me a good girl," but this time I added to myself, "so Papa will leave me with Aunt Anna forever and ever."

So I prayed night after night, and as day followed day I was still in New Bedford. Nothing was said about my returning to East Thompson, and about the middle of September Aunt Anna dressed me in my blue cashmere and my frilled white pinafore and told me I was to go to school. Though I felt some fear as to what might befall me, I said nothing about it but skipped along jauntily with my hand in hers.

The schoolmistress was a gentlewoman whose saintly soul was reflected in a manner so gentle and loving that the wildest of her pupils became lamblike beneath her gaze. She taught us as Miss Mary taught little Rollo,[2] and we loved her teaching. With "Seven Little Sisters"[3] we roamed over the whole earth. We had to know all there was to know about Europe because Jeanette and Louise lived there; and about Asia because of Pen-se; and about Africa because of Manenko and Gemila. The place I loved best and longed most to see, and the longing is still with me, unsatisfied, was the desert of Sahara. I am sure Gemila, that delightfully free soul, still lives under the shadow of the black tent. Some day I might meet her and we shall "sit outside the tent and enjoy the evening and the mother will bring to us dates and little hard cakes of bread with plenty of butter made from goat's milk."

We learned to read and at the same time to love poetry, from Coventry Patmore's *Children's Garland*. Of course, there were some poems that we were expected to skip, but I read them all, and rather shocked my gentle aunt by telling her I could not understand the one about "La Belly Dam Sangs Mercy." Young Lochinvar was my favorite.[4] Like him, I longed to go into the *West* and ride and ride, and one day I did.

Martha Russell, this well-beloved teacher, always dressed after the Puritan fashion, in a black, tight-fitting cashmere basque and a plain straight cashmere skirt, which touched the ground, her black cloth boots all hidden but the tips. Her dark brown hair, smooth as silk, was parted in the middle, and brought down over her ears. Her narrow collar and cuffs were white as the chalk with which we did our sums on the blackboard.

My mother, said Aunt Anna, had gone to school with Martha Russell. She loved the things she taught, and her earnestness was never styled as priggish, nor was her idealism termed old-maidish. Somewhere beyond the gate that closes upon the fields of this life's last great adventure, in a little gray schoolhouse with clean little desks and chairs, I feel that Martha Russell is still teaching a happy company of children to search unceasingly for beauty, to speak kindly, and to love truth.

About three o'clock every afternoon, Uncle Walton harnessed old Charley to the carryall and took Grandma and Aunt Anna and me for a drive. Sometimes we went to the "Head of the River," sometimes to Fairhaven, or again to the "Point." At the Head of the River the road crossed the stream over an old gray stone bridge, under which the dark waters murmured mysteriously. I used to wonder where the river's head was and what it looked like, but I kept this wonderment to myself. At Fairhaven there was a fort with a grassy embankment, a tall white beacon, and many rocks covered with sea grapes and barnacles. The

Edith Guerrier's uncle and aunt, Walton and Anna Ricketson, in his studio, admiring his bust of George William Curtis. The Ricketsons, brother and sister, served as surrogate parents for Edith. Reproduced courtesy of the Whaling Museum, New Bedford, Massachusetts.

Point road, white with the dust of countless clamshells, ran between low stone walls till it came to a full stop at the open sea. One day, when the pink wild roses were filling the air with their fragrance, and the blue waters were kissing the crisp yellow sands, and the gulls were writing poems in the air with their wings, I laughed aloud as we rode along for I knew that I should never see anything lovelier if I lived to be as old as Grandma.

"What are you laughing at, little Edie?" asked Uncle Walton, and I looked into his eyes and said, "Because," and he looked into mine and read the poem that I could not put into words.

My uncle Walton loved the waterfront, with its grass-grown wharves, where lay many old whaling vessels reminiscent of the days when New Bedford had been the foremost whaling port of the world. One day we climbed aboard one of the old ships and saw the big iron kettles wherein the whale blubber was tried out. We went into the captain's cabin where there was a gigantic swinging bunk with carved mahogany sides. Then we descended, down, down, down into the hold where the sailors had slept in narrow boxes along the sides. As we entered there was a noise like the rustling of paper, and as my uncle struck a match in the darkness I saw an army of black beetles about the size of small mice scurrying about.

The winter after I had come back to my own people, my grandmother fell ill and died. At first I could not understand how the house was to go on without her because, in spite of her invalidism and her calm and unhurried manner, we all recognized that Grandma was the head of the house. However, Aunt Anna had carried out her mother's wishes for so many years that she knew what Grandma would do under any circumstances, and her going left merely a ripple on the surface of our lives. We had our meals as regularly as ever, breakfast at half past seven, dinner at one, supper at half past six. Every morning I went to school; every fine afternoon Uncle Walton took Aunt Anna and me for a drive. Grandpa, according to his usual custom, was visible only at mealtimes. He had his own sitting room and bedroom on the ground floor, and there, when he was not eating his meals or taking a walk, he spent his days. After Grandma's death he rarely spoke, but if I spoke or laughed he would look at me from under his eyebrows in a manner that reminded me of Uncle Fox in the pulpit. One day, when I was feeling very naughty, I looked back at him and made what I called a monkey face, and stuck out my tongue.

"Anna," said Grandpa, in a terrible voice, "you are spoiling that child."

He said many more things, which I do not remember, and after dinner sweet Aunt Anna went into Grandma's room and wept. As for me, I did not weep. I made instant preparation to start for Fairyland! Two pairs of drawers, two pairs of stockings, two waists, two petticoats, my wrapper, and my bed shoes I bundled into a pinafore, tied the sleeves together, swung it all over my shoulder, after the picture of Christian in *Pilgrim's Progress*, and crept down the back stairs. As I was making my exit from the back door, Aunt Anna came hurrying through the kitchen. When she saw me and my bundle, she gathered me into her arms, bundle and all, and said, "You don't want to run away from Aunt Anna."

"No," I replied, "I want to run away from Grandpa."

Aunt Anna "reasoned" with me, but I remained obdurate. Finally she decided to let me go. With a scowl like Grandpa's worst, I started off. At the gate I paused, still frowning, and turned to look up at the window of my little room. Would I find one like it in Fairyland? Perhaps, after all, Aunt Anna was a fairy princess in disguise and Uncle Walton a fairy prince. Grandpa was a sure-enough ogre, but they would never let him eat me. I did not pass the gate but turned back and ran into the arms of my fairy-princess aunt. As for my bundle, it fell to the ground just as Christian's had done in the story.

Often on pleasant summer afternoons, instead of taking Aunt Anna and me for a drive, Uncle Walton took us for a sail in *Zephyr*, his open boat with two sails, which he kept tied to a pier somewhere near the old Wamsutta Mills. Frequently Mary Wall, daughter of William Wall, a New Bedford artist,[5] went with us.

Uncle Walton was not only an expert sailor but also an inimitable raconteur. Bobby Burns was his favorite poet, and he appeared to know by heart a complete volume of his poems. Sometimes when the breezes died and *Zephyr* was becalmed, he would draw Thoreau's flute from its linen case, woven and fashioned by Lydia Maria Child, and play "Flow Gently, Sweet Afton," "Annie Laurie," and other sweet, old-fashioned English and Scottish tunes. The flute had been given to him by Sophia Thoreau, sister of Henry Thoreau who, for many years before his death, had been Grandpa's most valued friend.

It was Uncle Walton who made me understand that books were the houses in which many charming and lovable persons, as well as fairies, lived. My favorite volume was a very large and unwieldy copy of *Don Quixote* illustrated with Doré woodcuts, from which I could read the story for myself of poor "Donkey Haughty," as I called him. *Hiawatha* was another favorite. There were no illustrations in that book, so while Uncle Walton read aloud, I made the pictures. Sometimes, instead of reading, he took me on his knee and told true stories about animals, birds, and fishes. He succeeded in teaching me to have kindly feelings toward all animals, excepting earthworms and snakes.

Uncle Walton never talked down to me. He seemed to feel that what interested him would interest me. He shared with me his memories of the man who had helped to make his own youth rich. The gentle Henry Thoreau, the princely George William Curtis, the benign Bronson Alcott, the inspired Ralph Waldo Emerson, and a score of literary men of the day, all friends of Grandfather's, who had spent well-remembered hours at Brooklawn with Daniel Ricketson and his sons and daughters.

The summer after Grandma's death, Aunt Anna and Uncle Walton rented a tiny cottage at Nonquitt, on the shore of Buzzards Bay, some six miles from New Bedford. Two features of the interior I can see with my mind's eye as clearly as I saw them more than seventy years ago: the beam, which ran around the dining room walls directly beneath the ceiling, bearing the painted legend, "The morning wind forever blows; the poem of creation is uninterrupted,"[6] and a huge fishnet spangled with barnacles, which veiled the roof of my uncle's studio.

In this studio he built me a little flat-bottomed boat called *The Mite* with the smallest pair of oars Nonquitters had ever seen. Every day while he shook out his sails aboard *Zephyr*, I rowed about in *The Mite*, proud as the captain of an ocean liner and fearless as the fishes.

Many a time, in the years since those halcyon days, I have dreamed of the Nonquitt cottage, set in the midst of a thicket of wild roses and honeysuckle, beside a cliff crowned with cedars of Lebanon. I have heard again the songs of many birds, the soft lapping of the waves against the cliffs, and the sound of my uncle's flute playing softly the airs he loved so well.

Papa came to see me once every month and told me that some day we would have a little house together, with books and pictures, and a lovely garden. I longed to be grown-up so that I could keep house for him, sit at the head of the table, manage the tea, go to market, and buy anything I fancied.

In my tenth year, the day before Christmas, Papa came as he always did on that day. After he had kissed me, instead of taking me for a walk, he went into Grandpa's study. I heard loud voices, which I remember well because I had never heard loud voices in that house before. At dinner everyone was very silent, and I could see that Aunt Anna had been crying. When the uncomfortable meal was over she took me by the hand and led me up to Grandpa's room. There she took me on her lap and kissed me many times. At last, in a trembling voice, she said, "Papa thinks you are now big enough to go and live with him, so you must be a good girl and not cry, and if you do just what he tells you, he will bring you to see Aunt Anna."

While the tears were still running down her cheeks, Papa entered with his watch in his hand. "Is she ready?" he asked.

"Why, no, George," said Aunt Anna, "I must pack her things."

"Never mind about her things," said my father, "I'll buy her some. Put on her hat and coat. We barely have time to catch the train."

Into the next two minutes Aunt Anna packed the tenderness that was to be the last I should experience for many years. She fondled the little coat she had made me before she slowly helped me into it; she kissed my eyes as she covered my curls with a white rabbit-skin cap; she kissed each hand as she drew on my mittens. Then Papa had me by the hand and was hurrying me down the street. I did not cry. I was going to be a good girl, but a sort of numbness came over me that I could not understand. It was like the fog that sometimes hid the shore when we were out sailing in Uncle Walton's *Zephyr*. I felt there was no sense in worrying because the fog had always lifted, and we had never failed to find a landing place.

It was snowing hard and fast as we boarded the train. My father seemed sad. The "Papa" days were over. Now, for the first time, I called him "Father" instinctively, and slid my hand into his.

"Father, where are we going?" I asked.

"To Aunt Fanny's in Boston," he replied.

"When are we going to our little house?"

"As soon as warm weather comes," he replied. "In the meantime, you are going to stay with Aunty Fox."

I saw that he did not want to talk and so I sat quite still watching the snow whirl past and praying, "O Lord, please make me a good girl so I can go back to my Aunt Anna."

Aunt Fanny's house was in the South End, in those days the genteel end of the town. The brick houses with "swell fronts," block after block of them, were all alike, very respectable, very uninteresting. The bay windows were crystal clear, but heavy damask curtains guarded the privacy of the interiors.

Even as a child I sensed the cold formality of the neighborhood. When the carved black walnut street door closed and I found myself standing in the heavily carpeted hallway, dimly lighted by one gas jet in a frosted globe, I was uncomfortably conscious that my copper-toed boots were very dusty, that a button had escaped from my coat, and that I had lost my handkerchief and one mitten. Aunt Fanny, in a stiff, shiny black dress, her sandy hair done "in water waves," said, "Well, this is unexpected, George," and gave him a "who let the cat in" look as she silently took off my hat and coat and hung them on the hat tree.

The room in which I had slept when I was a baby had not changed. I wished I were not too grown-up to sleep with Father, for the enormous four-poster, notwithstanding its mountainous feather bed, was very, very cold. It was Christmas eve, the time when for the past three years I had hung my stocking in front of the fireplace in Grandma's room, with full belief that Santa would fill it, and he had always done so. On this Christmas eve, in spite of the fact that I had been a good girl for at least a week and that Santa always remembered good girls, I was somewhat troubled as there was no fireplace in my room. I had such faith in Santa, however, that I thought, knowing how good I had been, he might come in at the window if I went to sleep at once. As soon as my father had taken away the lamp and I was left alone in the great damp bed in the black night, I crept out along the cold floor and secured a stocking, which I tied with a garter, to one of the bedposts. Then I jumped into the very middle of the big bed without saying my prayers, now that there was no Aunt Anna to remind me, covered my head with the bedclothes, and went to sleep. The first thing I saw in the morning was my stocking, limp and empty on the bedpost. I felt no resentment against Santa. I had proved that he entered by chimneys only.

We arrived before dinner at Mapleville, Rhode Island, the mill town where Uncle Fox now lived. Poor uncle, according to the rules of his church, was supposed to move into a new pasture every four years.[7] My father, having obtained from the depot master directions to the parsonage, took me by the hand and strode down the snowy road, past factories with smoking chimneys and wooden tenements which looked more like very old barns than human dwelling houses. As I trotted at a brisk pace, to keep up with him, I remarked that it was not a pretty street. My father did not ring the bell at the parsonage door, but walked right in, calling Aunty Fox's name. As usual she was in the kitchen working amid the cheerful odors of mincemeat, turkey, and onions. She hastily wiped her hands on her apron, took me in her arms, and kissed me, saying, "Well, George, this is indeed a surprise."

Uncle, Lizzie, and Susie greeted me with real affection; and no one seemed surprised that I was again to be a member of the family. After dinner, when my father left for Boston, I told Aunty about my empty stocking. She explained that probably Santa had brought my gifts in his sleigh with the other things for the tree at the church. Sure enough, there they were that evening, and, with greater faith than ever in dear Santa, I trudged home to the parsonage hugging to my breast a red stocking filled with the kind of toys Santa selects for those who live in mill villages. I was glad I had been good and had not blamed him.

Life at the Mapleville parsonage went on as at East Thompson, except that Susie had charge of me instead of Lizzie, who was now engaged to be married and consequently very busy dressmaking. I shared Susie's tiny unheated room, with the bedstead so placed under the eaves that one could not sit upright without bumping one's head. Again, I had dresses patched at the elbows, stockings darned everywhere, and drawers without ruffles.

As the minister's daughter, Susie lived to serve, and she gave with no thought of reward. Morning, noon, and night she cast bread upon the waters with never a prayer that it might return to her buttered. The sick of the parish besought her to come to them, the old and feeble begged her to read to them, and the young and gay found no party complete without her. She was one of the most useful and popular persons I have ever known.

As my father wished me to go to school while at Uncle Fox's, I went with fifty mill children to a tiny white schoolhouse on the peak of a steep little hill. My teacher was no Martha Russell. She taught loudly, emphatically, and vigorously—rules, dates, and capital cities. Opportunities for testing the usefulness of these facts were never offered. Over the blackboard, on a white strip of cardboard, were the six-inch letters, MYOB. I thought it some sort of magic key, like "open sesame," and was shocked beyond measure to find that it was the motto of the school, with the letters standing for the words, *Mind your own business.*

At home I learned to wash dishes and make beds, and at school I learned to mind my own business in the crowd of handkerchiefless mill children. My father wrote to me every week, but seldom came to see me, as Uncle Fox's house was so tiny it boasted no guest room. In all of his spare time Father was busy preparing a home for me and for his sister, a certain mysterious Aunt Margaret who was coming from England to live with us.

Early in the spring, Father came to Mapleville to take me to this home in Concord, Massachusetts. I could have wept bitterly at parting from Aunty Fox and Susie, but with dry eyes I said good-bye as jauntily as I could and went off with never a backward look. To outward appearances I was fast becoming "unfeeling."

When I saw Aunt Margaret, I thought she looked exactly like the pictures of Queen Victoria, except that she wore no crown. Perhaps because she had been an English schoolmarm, she set out most conscientiously to "bring me up." There was a rule for every action; every hour of the day had its duty; and a duty undone meant a punishment of some sort. I was a clumsy child who just naturally tore and broke things. Aunt Anna and Susie had pitied me for this and had lovingly tried to help me. Aunt Margaret took the attitude that I did such things on purpose and devised crude punishments. I remember spilling some mustard on someone's slippers and being made to wipe it up with my bath sponge, which so humiliated me that I still recall the incident.

During the summer Aunt Margaret brought me up vigorously and conscientiously. Sunday was, as it had been at East Thompson and Mapleville, a day to be looked forward to with gloomy forebodings and looked back upon with loathing and dismay. We walked three miles along a dusty road to church and then three miles back. During the dinner hour, which was given over to discussion of the sermon, I was seen and not heard. After dish washing was over, I stood and went through the catechism with Aunt Margaret. She began by asking, "What is your name?"[8]

The first Sunday I answered according to the book, "*N or M*," and was made to stand for ten minutes in the corner, face to the wall, because I had been impertinent. By four o'clock on every Sunday that followed, I was in a frame of mind to kick the cat, to cut out bunches of my hair, or to mix salt with the sugar; and the day usually ended by my being sent to bed supperless before dark.

By the fall, Aunt Margaret considered me so intractable that she refused to teach me any longer and sent me to the Concord Public School. What was my joy one morning, as I was scuffing along through the dead leaves toward the schoolhouse, to meet Aunt Anna face to face, and to learn that she and Uncle Walton had come to Concord to live. Grandpa Ricketson, she told me, had been very lonesome after Grandma's death and had brought home another grandma, and so my dear aunt and uncle had come to Concord to be near me. Papa had said, she told me, that if I were a good girl I might go to see her every Saturday afternoon. Thenceforward I was a reformed character, and I lived only for Saturday afternoons.

"My second home," as Aunt Anna called the house in which she and Uncle Walton lived, was on the bank of the river. Beside the water was a charming little canoe house with a red canoe, built by my uncle, in which I was to spend many joyous afternoons.

Aunt Anna's two dearest friends in Concord were Anna Pratt, the Meg of *Little Women*, and Louisa Alcott, the Jo of the same story. One afternoon Aunt Anna was on her way to call on Louisa when I espied her on my way home from school and ran after her. Of course she could not resist the temptation of giving her little niece the opportunity of seeing the beloved author of *Little Women*. When we got to the door Aunt Anna discovered that my hands were very dirty. In spite of that, Louisa, who came to the door herself, looked at me kindly and seemed to think it was a most natural thing for little girls to have dirty hands. I remember being taken to "May's room," where I was cleaned up. I also remember wondering about certain pencil drawings "right on the walls." My aunt explained to me on the way home that the drawings had been done by May (I knew her as Amy), who was no longer living, and that they would never be erased. The drawings did not seem to me very wonderful. I was quite sure I could do as well, but I had no expectation of dying, and that being the case, I reasoned, I'd better not decorate my bedroom walls.

One Saturday afternoon I found Aunt Anna at work in the kitchen. She explained that Uncle Walton's friend, "Dan French," had sent over to borrow Lizzie [her maid] and some teaspoons, as he was having a little tea party in his studio.

At suppertime Uncle Walton told me about his friend, Daniel Chester French, the sculptor; and one not-to-be-forgotten afternoon I was taken to his studio, a small inconspicuous cottage, some distance from the road, in a broad field. It was quite filled with pictures, busts, and statues, but I remember only the white marble Endymion, so placed that the lighting brought out the ethereal beauty of the young sculptor's poetic conception.

On an afternoon when Concord was embosomed in apple blossoms and lilacs, purple and white, and all the air was sweet with the scent of flowers, my uncle and I paddled down the river, which he always called the *Musketaquid*,⁹ that being the Indian word for "grass-grown river." On the right bank green lawns sloped gently to the water, and gardens gay with tulips, jonquils, larkspur, and many other old-fashioned flowers lay like oriental carpets spread before the fine old colonial mansions, each one of which had its small canoe house, for the river was in those distant days the town's Grand Canal. On the east bank, in green pastures, cattle drowsed in the shade of graceful elms. The river on that side was fringed by alders, and where there was a stray boulder my uncle would hand me Thoreau's spyglass and tell me to look for a painted turtle and count till I had seen ten—no difficult task, for the river abounded in those gay-coated creatures. When we were abreast of the old gray manse, my uncle paused and pointed with his paddle across the river where, on the left bank, at the end of a rude bridge, stood the Minute Man, the work of Daniel Chester French, his sculptor friend. I looked long at the gallant figure, and "I should like to be a Minute Man," I told my uncle.

On a Saturday when the river was white with water lilies and the pastures were gay with wild roses and crowfoot violets, we paddled to Fairhaven Bay, pausing often to watch the red-winged blackbirds skimming from bank to bank. "Thoreau," my Uncle said, "knew this part of the river better than he knew his own dooryard. He was more intimately acquainted with flowers, birds, and beasties than with his human neighbors."

My uncle never said "Mr. Thoreau," or "Henry Thoreau," but always "Thoreau" (*Thaw-'row* he pronounced it, for that is the way Thoreau himself pronounced it, he said). My uncle also knew the birds and flowers. "Listen," he would whisper, "that is a song sparrow, hear how he says '*Maids, maids, maids, hang on your tea kettle-ettle-ettle-ettle-ettle.*' A very nice song but rather foolish words"; or, "There is the wood thrush who says, according to Mr. Ralph Waldo Emerson, '*Heigh, Willy-Willy—Heigh, Willy-Willy-Willy-O.*'" A moment later he rested his paddle in the water and silently nodded toward a clump of rushes among which there was a slight movement, and for a breathtaking moment a stately blue kingfisher emerged, stood still, and then flashed like blue lightning across the river.

As we turned into Fairhaven Bay, which seemed like a lake in the midst of the river, a clumsy muskrat slithered through the elder bushes and plumped into the water. "Many of these beasties have channeled mansions along the banks," remarked my uncle. On the sandy shore of Fairhaven Bay we landed long enough for Uncle Walton to gather a nosegay of wild roses for "the sister." When she was not with him he never returned from a walk or canoe trip without some offering—flowers, or a brilliant shell, or maybe a handful of wild strawberries in a bark cup lined with leaves or moss.

On pleasant winter afternoons my uncle strapped on my feet a beautiful pair of skates that he had made, with highly polished curly-maple soles, and blades that swirled up past my toes like the skates in pictures of *Hans Brinker and the Silver Skates*.[10] Then he pulled me on a sled down to the river and taught me to stand alone, and to skate. When I was tired he skated and pushed me before him over the ice in a high-backed sledge he had made. At six o'clock, glowing with health and happiness, we went back to the house where Aunt Anna awaited us in the living room, which was always gay with hemlock and red berries. Here we sat before the cheery open fire till the tea bell sounded. At seven o'clock Aunt Margaret came for me, and I would begin to count the hours till next Saturday.

At the end of a winter of Saturdays, for those were the only days that counted, Aunt Margaret, like Grandpa, became lonesome and went to England—"to get another husband," as I explained to Aunt Anna. My poor father was quite broken-hearted, as he had completely furnished the little cottage on Academy Hill Road and had looked forward with hope and joy to making it a permanent home for his sister and his little daughter.

My next stopping place was in Brookline, Massachusetts, in what was known as a private boardinghouse, kept by a charming lady and her daughters. Every morning at eight o'clock my father went off to his office in Boston, and at half past eight I went to the public school. I was then eleven years old and felt quite able to take care of myself, as well as of my father who was unfailingly kind and patient. One of his business associates, Mr. Jenney, whose home was just around the corner, had a large-hearted wife who was not so sure that I was fully capable of bringing myself up. Every day after school she invited me to come to her house until my father got home. Her three boys soon seemed to me like brothers.

While we were in Brookline, Uncle Eben, one of my father's half-brothers, came from England to America, ill and without funds—a circumstance, however, which did not prevent him from falling in love with a pretty young girl, also penniless. A few days after their marriage he told my father all about it. Now my father was of a romantic turn himself, and, instead of chiding his brother, he borrowed quite a sum of money and bought for the young couple a small farm in Pepperell, Massachusetts. As soon as Uncle Eben and his wife were settled, we began to spend our weekends there, and sometimes the entire Jenney family accompanied us. Then what fun we had.

Not far from our farm was a hill densely wooded to within thirty feet of the bare, flat top known as "the Pinnacle." One evening, when the October moon hung low in the heavens, we prepared for a corn roast on the Pinnacle. Mr. Jenney, who had a keen sense of humor, insisted that since a corn roast was one of the earliest of New England festivities, we should be as old-fashioned as possible. He had discovered a carriage shop behind which a dozen or more old vehicles were slowly falling to pieces; and with the consent of the carriage maker and with the help of the men of the party, some of these were tinkered up a bit, horses were hitched to them, and thus conveyances suitable to the occasion were provided. I can still see one very stout old New England dame climbing into an ancient barouche and stepping right through the floor of the vehicle. Her fat, white-clad legs were visible to the knees under the carriage, and she stood with her bonnet over one eye, seeking helplessly to pull her dress down. It took the combined efforts of four men to haul her out of the debris, while two more held the horses.

How good the damp leaves smelled as we climbed up through the woods, and how like it was to the volcanoes in my geography book, when we first saw the glowing smoke of the wood fire ascending to the sky. When the corn had been roasted to a turn, when I had grasped a yellow ear and sunk my teeth into the golden kernels, I experienced such a sense of well-being and contentment that the Pinnacle even now seems to me a sort of Olympus upon which, for a brief space, we became as gods.

After a few months in Brookline, my father, dissatisfied with his progress in a Boston insurance office, decided to go to Chicago and start again in the Chicago, Burlington, and Quincy Railroad offices, where he had worked directly after the Civil War. He could not leave me at the boardinghouse in Brookline, but there was always Aunty Fox to fall back upon. Uncle Fox, who was now in his seventieth year, had recently been sent to preach at Pocasset on Cape Cod. The parsonage to which I was sent was a tiny white house on a hilltop opposite the white church. From this hill one could look across the water to Wing's Neck, which ended in a small headland on which stood a lighthouse whose steady light shone like a fixed star from sunset to sunrise.

As a parting gift my father had presented me with a golden-brown, shirred satin dress with ruffled skirt and a little basque that ended back and front in sharp points. It was trimmed with cut steel buttons. My father was extremely proud of this purchase, but I beheld it with utmost dismay. When I wore the thing to church and sat between Aunty Fox and Susie in their decent, plain alpaca gowns, I felt the eyes of the congregation fixed upon me. I longed to explain that I was not the vain and affected piece the dress proclaimed me to be. But who would have believed me? I never saw a dress with such wearing qualities. It developed in me a hatred of fine clothes, which I have never overcome, and an aversion for attending church services which I have had to resist for many years.

The parsonage soon seemed to me like home. On the sitting room floor was the same green Brussels carpet with red spots, which I had seen at East Thompson and at Mapleville. In one corner stood Susie's organ, under the window was the haircloth sofa with bumpy springs, and on a stand in another corner was the big family Bible with its bookmark, which I considered a remarkable curiosity. It was a small double hand with pointing index finger made of metal thin as paper. Uncle Fox always used it to mark the place where he left off in reading the Scripture lesson, which he rendered with dramatic intensity. I can never be sufficiently grateful to him for providing me with a knowledge of biblical literature, which has stood me in good stead on many an occasion.

In his youth the Reverend Samuel Fox had a longing to go to sea. As his father had no sympathy with his desire, he left home and went to a seaport town, where he shipped as a common sailor on a whaling vessel bound for the polar seas. He experienced his conversion," and Susie, "in the mouth of a whale." "You see," she explained, "he was out in the jolly boat following a whale, when that great Leviathan, as the Bible calls him, turned on his pursuers and took the boat in his jaws. As my father passed through the mouth of the whale, he vowed that if Almighty God would save him, he would spend the rest of his life praising Him. God did save him, and he kept his promise. The first port he made was New Bedford. There he went to the Seamen's Bethel and told his story, declaring that he wished to spend his life preaching the greatness and power of God."

This story explained certain of Uncle Fox's idiosyncracies that had puzzled me. He was, I saw now, nautical through and through. His voice in the pulpit was that of the captain on the bridge. His church was his ship, his home his cabin, and he was supreme in each, responsible only to the owner under whom he had shipped and to whom he was bound to deliver a cargo of souls.

Every morning immediately after breakfast we went to the sitting room for prayers. I always made for the haircloth sofa and, as Uncle Fox read, I stole furtive glances at the outside world. When he prayed I had the great advantage, as I knelt, of facing the scenery. In winter the fields, smoothly blanketed with untrodden snow, sloped down to the glassy surface of the frozen bay. The houses, few and far between, no longer hidden behind screens of lilac bushes, stood forth stark and lonesome. The distant lighthouse, white as the snow, was hardly visible on the edge of the gray and white landscape, silent save for the occasional jingle of the bells on the fish peddler's pung or on the baker's covered sledge.

In the spring and early summer I could see on the long green hill splashes of crowfoot violets, yellow cinquefoil, and blue-and-white houstonia known as "stars of innocence." Gray cottages were nested in clumps of foliage, fragrant with lilac and syringa blossoms. The lighthouse, the foam, and the clouds were foils for the blueness of sea and sky. Robins sang joyously, and chimney swallows slipped up and down before the window, sweeping the air with their flashing wings.

Fall was the time of herring runs. From where I knelt I could see at the foot of the hill the Red Brook House where the brook ran under the road on its way to the cove. I could see in my mind's eye the fishermen, with trousers rolled above their sea boots, standing knee-deep in the water, scooping out the herring with their nets and flinging the silvery fishes upon the bank till hundreds, if not thousands, had accumulated in a great shining heap.

After the Scripture reading was over, there were always dishes to be wiped. During the winter season, I started out well wrapped up, my strap of books in one red-mittened hand, and my tin luncheon pail in the other. The district school was about a mile away down the hill, through a farmhouse yard, and along the high road. The teacher, a graduate of an "elocution school," aspired to be an actress. She had us give recitations continually. I learned *The Wreck of the Hesperus*,[11] with appropriate inflections and gestures, and wished that I might display my dramatic ability to my dear old teacher, Miss Martha Russell, who had never made a gesture or raised her voice, or sighed, or moaned, or roared, as long as I had known her.

At noontime those of us who had brought our luncheons sat around the "depot stove," which heated the room, and swapped eatables. A few of the older girls hurried through their luncheons in order that they might tie tags, a favorite Cape Cod industry. Once a week the tag woman arrived in the village in a democrat wagon,[12] drawn by a sleek brown horse. The body of the wagon was filled with brown cloth sacks containing tags in bundles of one hundred and pink strings in bundles of one hundred. Most persons took several thousands of these. They then proceeded to thread a pink string through the eye of each tag, knotting the string about a fourth of an inch from the ends. The tags, when strung, were gathered in bunches of one hundred and tied. For each hundred tags the worker received one cent. The financial deals put through by tag tying were amazing. A red carpet was purchased that covered the church aisle from door to pulpit. Mortgages were lightened, and missionaries were assisted.

The arrival of the tag woman, all in brown, with her brown bags, her brown wagon, and brown horse, was an expected and unquestioned occurrence. It seemed that she, like the brook, must go on forever. Yet I am told that machinery snatched the tag-tying industry from the hands of the Cape Codders, and that in consequence the tag woman, all in brown, with her brown horse and her brown wagon, ceased to be a figure on Cape Cod roads.

This may all be true, yet recently while walking along the road from Pocasset to Monument Beach, in the dusk of evening, I certainly saw the whole brown outfit—horse, wagon, tag woman, and bags—pass me, skimming along about a foot above the ground. I paused and called out, "Tag woman, ahoy!" She did not even turn her head, and as I stood looking at the well-remembered vehicle, it gradually melted into the elusive shadows of evening.

Another of those Cape Cod industries that still survives is cranberry picking. Down the hill behind the parsonage was a bog, silent during the greater part of the year, save for an occasional whistling laborer; tenantless, save for the pickerel in the tiny canals that divided the bog into blocks. But on spring evenings frogs made the whole air shrill with their pipings. Then, in the fall, all was different. The marshes, with millions of crimson berries, were invaded by an army of pickers in colorful costume, swaying to and fro, and as they moved slowly forward the vines were denuded and the berries fell into great wooden measures in rattling showers.

It was of no use to open school till cranberry season was over, as all the children were on the bogs working with their parents. Cranberry picking was not one of my chores, although I wished heartily that it were, as most of the tasks assigned me seemed astonishingly prosaic. It was my duty to wipe dishes, do patch work, make beds, and go for the milk. The last job was one that tested my courage to the utmost.

Every evening immediately after supper I started for the milk farm, which was about half a mile from the parsonage, across the fields and through the woods. Going, I jingled the pail to keep myself company; returning, with my quart of milk, I had to go slowly. The evening I remember most distinctly was in the latter part of April. I had stopped on the way to gather arbutus, and dusk had fallen as I emerged from the belt of scrub pines between the milk farm and the Freeman place. Now the Freeman place was a lonesome spot at best, even if one did not know its story. The weather-beaten old farmhouse, surrounded by its ramshackle outbuildings, stood in a small cleared hollow, a perfect bowl of a place, sunken as it were in the earth, rimmed with acre upon acre of scrub pines.

The house had been deserted ever since Mr. and Mrs. Freeman, two religious fanatics, had slain their six-year-old child who, like myself, was named Edith. Given the setting, it was impossible not to reconstruct the tragedy. The man, creeping toward the sleeping child with sharp, shining knife, the wife holding the lamp aloft, then, twenty or more members of their sect stealthily arriving at the house and assembling around the dead child's bed, with profound conviction that she would arise in response to their prayers; the final discovery of the tragedy, and the burial of the unrisen child. These scenes haunted my memory each time I passed the house.[13]

On this particular evening, of which I am writing, the full moon appeared amid swiftly scudding fleets of clouds. In the curtainless windows of the house lights seemed to dance, and a strange shadow began walking beside me along the trail. Regardless of the slopping milk, I turned, ran up the side of the hollow, through the next belt of pines, and past the graveyard with its gleaming rows of stones, among which lay buried a murdered child. Once out on the highroad, with the lights of the parsonage before me, I felt safe again. Still panting, I questioned myself. Why could I not remember at the proper time that even though I walked through the valley of the shadow of death, God was with me? I was safe, I had spilled only a little milk, and I should not have to go that way again for twenty-four hours. With a jaunty air I walked into the kitchen, set down my pail, and hurried to get my Sunday-school book for the half hour of reading allowed me before bedtime.

Evening after evening, thereafter, for many months I shuddered through Freeman Hollow, trembled as I skirted the graveyard, and regained my courage on the highroad. Even in the midst of my terror, I could never bring myself to promise that if God would protect me I would become a preacher, a missionary, or some other holy person. It would not have been a square deal, for I knew I could not make good at any of these jobs. I just asked Him to protect me because I was small and terrified, and of course He did.

One evening as I set my milk pail on the table I was told that "Aunt" Mary Handy's friend who stayed with her had been suddenly called home and that I would have to go and sleep at Aunt Mary's house. Now Aunt Mary Handy's house was a few paces down the hill at the edge of the graveyard. Aunt Mary was deaf as a post, lame as an old horse, and afflicted with a cough like the chug-chug of a locomotive pulling a freight train. I did not covet the honor of protecting her. However, Uncle Fox quoted, "Even as ye have done it unto one of the least of these . . . ," so I rolled my brush, comb, and toothbrush in my nightgown, kissed Uncle and Aunty and Susie good-night, ran down the hill to the lilac-hidden cottage, and knocked loudly on the door. Aunt Mary opened it, peering at me through her steel-rimmed spectacles. She was a tall, angular old lady with a tanned, sea-captainish face. Her voice was hoarse, and deep. Knowing her deafness, I shrieked that I had been sent to spend the night with her.

"Thank you, child, thank you," she growled, "come right in."

She led me quickly through the tiny hall to a bedroom which contained a four-poster as large as the one I still remembered in Aunt Fanny's house on Harrison Avenue in Boston.[14] There she left me, having first lighted a candle which she set on the washstand. I undressed quickly and folded the white spread as I had been taught to do. I was delighted with the patchwork quilt, just pink-and-white squares, nothing else. I had never seen one before with so few colors. In the shadowy room with its brown wallpaper, its furniture dark as only very old, unpolished mahogany can be, that quilt looked like a garden of pink-and-white roses. The scent of real roses, however, did not hang around it. For those who have slept in a musty feather bed, I need not describe the smell that assailed my nostrils. For those who have never had this experience, it would be useless to try to compare to any known odor an emanation that is like nothing but itself. While I was still trying to arrange my head so that I should be as far as possible from the feather tick, Aunt Mary began to cough. Just as the heavy freight engine coughs while pulling its long line of coal cars up a mountain, so Aunt Mary coughed. Like the engine she made a business of coughing. She did it thoroughly, displaying breath control that any opera singer might have coveted.

Her first long-drawn hoot brought me to a sitting position and took me out of immediate contact with the feathers. I could breathe more easily. At first I thought I should go to the aid of Aunt Mary, but as I became accustomed to the performance, I realized that it was a harmless habit, and with the discovery that Aunt Mary's cough was an innocuous, if not a sociable, effort, I fell asleep sitting up against the headboard, not to waken till called by Aunt Mary herself.

I had been told to go home to breakfast, but when I beheld a plate of crisp, brown doughnuts and a tempting, fat custard pie on the table, it needed no urging on Aunt Mary's part to persuade me to remain. Aunty Fox considered it quite a breach of good manners on my part to have put Aunt Mary to the trouble of giving me breakfast. "She was tempted by luxurious food," said Susie.

One more picture I must wipe clear of cobwebs before I leave the Cape, that of a Cape Cod clambake of more than half a century ago. It was the kind of get-together in which the entire community took part. Some rode in wagons, some walked to the chosen spot, a clump of pines on a knoll overlooking Buzzards Bay. The men of the party were the official cooks. First they dug a deep hole, in which a fire was made. When this was blazing well and there was a good body of live coals, a pile of stones was thrown in. When these were well heated, they were covered with damp eelgrass on which the clams were placed. On the clams more eelgrass was thrown, and on the eelgrass more clams, until near the top of the hole corn and sweet potatoes were substituted for clams. On top of the last layer of eelgrass, boards were laid.

While the clams, corn, and sweet potatoes were cooking, other eatables were displayed on white tablecloths by each party that arrived. I use the word *displayed* advisedly. Never since have I seen such a varied and interesting collection of cakes and pies. There were plain cakes, pink, white, yellow, and brown frosted cakes; marble, plum, blueberry, angel, pound, and layer cakes. There were squash, apple, cherry, prune, custard, cranberry, peach, rhubarb, mince, and apple pies. Of preserves, the kinds were many and varied. Of sandwiches, the only varieties were cheese, ham, chicken, corned beef, and plain bread and butter. Promptly at twelve noon the male cooks announced that the clams, corn, and potatoes were done to a turn, and each group arranged itself on the soft pine needles around a tablecloth piled high with food. Uncle Fox then asked a blessing on the food about to be consumed and, being subject himself to violent attacks of indigestion, begged the Almighty to grant us a peaceful termination of our warfare upon the various commodities spread before us. Then we fell upon the food with a vigor worthy of such a cause, leaving as a tangible monument to our accomplishment a sizable pile of clamshells, and corncobs.

As on the night of the corn roast, I felt completely satisfied with myself and the world and, judging by appearances, everyone else felt the same. I saw people laughing and talking together who had been known as sworn enemies. I, myself, spoke kindly to a little girl who had insulted me by calling me "moon face." Uncle Fox patted on the back a young woman whom he had rebuked from the pulpit for laughing in church. Holding a corn roast or a clambake in season can save a community the expense of lawsuits.

I now looked upon Uncle, Aunty, and Susie as my proper family. Yet every Tuesday when I had a letter from my father, filled with wise and loving counsel and with frequent mention of the time when I should be old enough to keep house for him, I was reminded that I was really only an adopted member of this family.

One morning, in place of his usual letter, he himself appeared at the parsonage about ten o'clock. Not content to wait until I got home from school, he went after me, and finding the door of the schoolroom closed, he opened it, poked in his head, and shouted, "Edith!" When he withdrew his head, the entire room broke into laughter, led by the teacher, and, feeling myself forever disgraced, I ran out into my father's arms with half the joy of his homecoming blotted out for the moment. I did not go back to ask the teacher's permission to absent myself for the rest of the day. I took my hat and lunch pail from my hook in the little front porch, grasped my father's hand, and with a hop, skip, and jump left the Pocasset District School for what proved to be the last time.

There seem to be many last times in this story, but a last time for one place inevitably meant a first time for another.

"Moving about," said my father, "prevents a person from getting set in her ways."

I had always associated the word *set* with a hen's business. Uncle Fox had several dozen fine Plymouth Rock fowls in a tidy yard behind the house, and I knew if the hen was not "set," there would be no eggs hatched into fluffy chickens. My father was correct in his statement. This running about from one school to another—New Bedford, Mapleville, Concord, Brookline, and Pocasset, in the space of three years— had made it impossible for me to sit on any batch of ideas long enough to hatch them. Perhaps that was why I remained poor in everything the schools taught except geography. I realized dimly that this was not my father's meaning, but, like most children, I smiled at my elders and silently arrived at my own conclusions.

TWO

Father and Daughter,

1883–1891

 Four days from the time I had so suddenly and unexpectedly left my school we were at Niagara Falls. Goat Island was then in a natural state; flowers grew in wild profusion, and we wandered at will through perfect jungles of untrimmed underbrush, till we came to the shore and the Falls, which I had expected to be four times as high. If, however, their appearance was disappointing, their roar was entirely satisfactory.

Hours later we were in Chicago, the roar of which seemed to me even greater than that of Niagara. My father had lodgings in a suburb called Riverside, with a Miss Marjorie J. Summers who wrote for the magazines. I looked up a story of hers the other day in an old *Harper's Bazaar*, and it brought back to me quite clearly the picture of my first day at her house.

Immediately after breakfast, which the boarders, some twelve men, consumed audibly and with incredible rapidity, they started down the road running at top speed. After Miss Summers had watched them for a moment, she began to carry the breakfast dishes into the kitchen. I asked if I might help, whereupon I was given the grayest and dingiest dish towel I had ever seen. The dishes disposed of, Miss Summers went upstairs to tidy the men's rooms. One bed she threw together, one set of slops she emptied, her motions becoming more and more dreamy. Then she unbelted her Mother Hubbard, seated herself at a small ink-spattered desk and began to write furiously with a pen, which spluttered black foam and made creaking sounds as it left irregular trails on one huge sheet of foolscap after another.

I interested myself by making beds, stopping to read bits from the books which I found scattered everywhere. I cannot recall what happened at lunchtime. I do remember that late in the afternoon Miss Summers arose, gathered up her papers, and dashed upstairs. Dashed is really not the right word, for she was a massive woman, fleshy but not muscular, whose motions were clumsy, and whose rapid progress was achieved by a series of lunges, frequently resulting in broken glass, china, and furniture.

She was most grateful to me for making the beds and, after emptying more slops, she stormed the kitchen, took by force the foodstuffs she could lay her hands on, and with the aid of her imagination, without benefit of cookbook, she evolved a dinner. Instead of spoons for mixing, she used her hands, snatching and throwing together handfuls and pinches of various dry commodities. Upon these she poured water or milk, stirring the entire mass with her hands, which became quite clean in the process. The results were unusual, but very good. She satisfied "her boys," as she termed her boarders, by providing them with an unlimited supply of gravy.

One of the boys was Miss Summers's brother, whose mind seemed to be elsewhere. He rarely spoke and seldom raised his eyes from his plate. A friend, whom I met some ten years later, told me that "Marjorie J." had opened this boardinghouse to make a pleasant home for her brother, a shiftless, idle, drunken fellow who, contrary to the moral endings of Sunday-school storybooks, remained shiftless, idle, and drunken all his days.

Just before my father had staged his first and only appearance at the Pocasset District School to retrieve me, he had received notice of his transfer from the Chicago to the Burlington, Iowa, office of the railroad. He therefore left me for several weeks at Riverside while he went ahead to find suitable lodgings. During that time I became quite fond of Miss Marjorie J. Summers, who "wrote for the magazines," and I corresponded with her thenceforward to the time of her death, about thirty years later.

In Burlington, we boarded with short, chubby, black-haired Mrs. Eldon, whose thin, quiet husband appeared to be her humble servant, even as she herself appeared to be the humble servant of a tiny, black-and-tan spaniel, who slept outside his mistress's bedroom door in a small pagoda with a white lamb's wool mat before it. This mite of a dog, who had his weekly bath standing on all fours in a hand washbasin, was a perfect watchdog. Let any other steps than those of his family be heard in the house and "Nippy" raised the roof. Soon we came to be such very good friends that many a night he burrowed under the covers of my bed and slept at my feet.

From the time my father went to his office in the morning until he returned in the evening, I was left to my own devices. I even ate my luncheon in solitary state. It was a concession for Mrs. Eldon to have taken a child into the house, but so long as I made no more trouble than the menfolks, she agreed to tolerate me.

Sunday mornings I went with my father to church; in the afternoon we walked miles and miles along the river or into the country between natural hedges of Osage orange and sunflowers nodding on stalks more than ten feet high. I missed the hills and woods of New England, with their ferns and wildflowers, but most of all, and more and more, I missed the dear home life with Aunt Anna and Uncle Walton.

On one of our walks, Father had with him a Mr. Crapo and his daughter, formerly of New Bedford. It was a happy Sunday for me. I had found a friend and thereafter I was made beautifully welcome at her home during the summer I spent in Burlington. Mary, like myself, was of an adventurous turn of mind. On that first Sunday she told me she had always wanted to explore the bluffs along the river where fossil shellfish, geodes, and feldspar could be found. Exploring the bluffs, therefore, became one of my favorite pastimes, and I still have in a cigar box fossils and bits of feldspar, which have always seemed so precious that I have never thrown them away.

One Saturday my father took me down the Mississippi on a riverboat. The stream seemed as wide as a lake and as brown as muddy coffee. The flat shores, which scarcely rose above the level of the water, were grassless and fernless, just hard, damp, black earth from which rose straight trunks of trees with foliage far above the ground.

"I thought," said I to my father, "it would be like the blue Juniata in the song."[1]

"And I thought, when I was your age," he replied, "that it would be like that with most of the animals one sees in a circus on its banks."

Then he told me that his father had taken him, when a little boy, to see a panorama of the Mississippi, flowing through beautiful tropical foliage in which monkeys leaped and played, and under which could be seen lions, leopards, and other animals of interest to hunters and to students of natural history. My father was neither, but he had an adventurous

Edith Guerrier's father, George Guerrier, in Civil War uniform as a 2nd lieutenant, 35th Regiment, U.S. Colored Troops. Reproduced courtesy of the Whaling Museum, New Bedford, Massachusetts.

spirit, and that picture of the Mississippi stayed with him until, at the age of nineteen, he gave up his position in the engineering department of the Great Western Railroad in London and sailed for America in search of adventures on the banks of the Mississippi River.

By fall, my father decided to go to his brother Sam, who was in the lumber business in Atchison, Kansas. He therefore placed me in a boarding school in Burlington. Very few children lived at the school, but there were a number of day pupils. Those of us who lived there were supposed to be members of the family. We ate at the family table and studied our lessons in the family sitting room, but at that point the relationship stopped. If we had colds, we got over them in our own way. If we had troubles, we cried about them in secret. If we wanted help, we consulted the Lord in the privacy of our closets.

I learned nothing at that school, excepting the conjugation of the verb *aimer* and the power of silence. This latter virtue was so impressed upon me that when I was thrown from my sled in coasting and broke a rib, I was so sure that this was the result of careless and unladylike behavior that I bore the injury in silence and, while my comrades coasted, remained in my room until my "rheumatism" was better.

At the end of the spring term, my father came to take me to Uncle Sam's. It had never occurred to me that any person other than the American gentleman in stovepipe hat, coat with starry tails, and trousers with red stripes could be called Uncle Sam. That my father's brother, an Englishman, should bear that name was a pleasant surprise. I learned some years later that he had come to America because of his marriage to an estimable young lady who was considered to be his social inferior. Having been told that there were no class distinctions in the United States, he thought it would be a happy place in which to raise a family.

We reached Atchison late in the evening. Uncle Sam, who met us at the station with a prancing horse and a smart little carriage, drove us home at a pace that reminded me of young Lochinvar, and though I was sadly in need of sleep, I was sorry when we arrived at his comfortable home in well-kept grounds.

Aunt Emma received us casually, surveyed me critically, and said, "She's very small for her age, isn't she?"

My father looked at me, appeared to notice this evident fact for the first time and said, "Yes, I suppose she is."

I had never thought anything about my size before, but this pointed observation from Aunt Emma made me conscious that I was smaller than I should be. However, I made up my mind then and there not to be sorry for myself, but to act as though I were as broad and as tall as the broadest and tallest person who might look down on me.

Because the children—George, John, Florence, and Beatrice—were all at a party, I did not make their acquaintance until the next morning when they wandered into breakfast one after another. In the six or more months I spent in Atchison, I cannot recall that the entire family sat down to a meal at the same time. George and John were young men in their twenties, employed in offices downtown. Florence and Beatrice, pretty girls of seventeen and nineteen, spent their days getting ready for the evenings when their young men called or when, about once in two weeks, they had a party.

On party nights the entire house was open excepting the servants' quarters, Uncle Sam's bedroom, the kitchen, and the "little back room." Into this out-of-the-way place was thrown everything we did not have time to mend, or to cleanse, or to dispose of properly. My refuge on party nights was under the little back room bed, a place safe rather than airy; so safe indeed that I was never discovered. Aunt Emma sought sanctuary in the kitchen with Minerva, the black cook. As for Uncle Sam, if he forgot himself so far as to come home from the office, he crept upstairs like a veritable Merdle,[2] and once in his bedroom, he locked and bolted the door.

My father had left Atchison the morning after our arrival for a frontier town in the southwestern part of the state, where Uncle Sam had recently opened a lumberyard. The building boom that struck Kansas in the eighties encouraged the opening of lumberyards everywhere and resulted in the financial ruin of many too trusting men who, like my father and my uncle, let the settler have the lumber on his promise to pay when he harvested his crops, sold his cattle, or disposed of his farm back east in Missouri.

Sometimes a debtor with a conscience endeavored to give value received by forfeiting his personal property. I recall one instance where a bookseller, who could not pay for the lumber with which his house was built, gave Uncle Sam, in part payment, several thousand volumes. Uncle Sam, who loved books, received the collection with joy and installed it on shelves built along the walls from one end to the other of the long parlors. Thereafter he never sat down to a meal without a book propped up in front of him. As for me, I spent my days curled up in a chair before the bookshelves reading indiscriminately. I went through entire sets of Dickens, Scott, Charlotte Brontë, and Thackeray and dipped into many volumes of poetry. I recall particularly my enjoyment of *Lalla Rookh*,[3] which bred in me a lasting attachment to the Vale of Kashmir. As there was no law in Kansas for the compulsory attendance at school of those under sixteen, I peacefully pursued my indiscriminate reading, independently.

During the winter months I went for a few hours each day to a business college where I was taught bookkeeping, business arithmetic, and Spencerian handwriting, with the idea that I might some day do the office work at my father's lumberyard.

There were no movies in those days and few good plays. I recall the excitement with which we heard that "Lotta"[4] was coming to Atchison. We thought of her as one of the greatest actresses in the world. In one scene of the play she jumped on a barrel and beat a tattoo upon it with her heels. I was particularly delighted to find that, though a very great actress, she was not "highbrow."

It was the habit of the young and old men, women, and children of Atchison to attend the Law Court. I gained my first knowledge of court procedure by sitting through the trial of a man who had murdered his wife in a singularly brutal manner. Toward the end of the trial, the courtroom was so crowded that we youngsters could not get in, but a friendly policeman who felt it a pity for us to lose the lesson that the judge's summing-up would teach us, let us in by a back door and permitted us to roost on a long table directly behind the judge, where we had a good view of the murderer and his weeping relatives. At this time I was as grown-up in my attitude toward men, women, and events as I am today. I had no guidance of any kind. I got up in the morning when I pleased, went to bed when the house was sufficiently quiet, asked Minerva the cook for my meals, quite as I would have done at a hotel, and told Aunt Emma when I needed new clothes. Uncle Sam was always kind when I spoke to him; otherwise he never noticed me. Aunt Emma was kind, but she made it quite apparent that I was not one of hers.

With regard to their own children, both Aunt Emma and Uncle Sam seemed to feel that parental responsibilities ended with giving them food, clothing, and enough spending money to enable them to entertain their friends freely. As to bringing them up, that was the children's own affair, and I must confess that they managed to bring themselves up creditably. All became model citizens with well-behaved children and, later, perfectly respectable grandchildren.

In the spring of 1886 my father arrived in Atchison to take me West with him. As I was nearly sixteen years of age, he felt that I was quite old enough to manage a house. The fact that I knew nothing about cooking and had had no experience in the performance of household duties, other than dish wiping, bed making, and dusting, had nothing to do with the case. I was going on sixteen, my father wanted me to keep his house, and I wanted the adventure of keeping it.

My father told me that he was having a beautiful little stone house built for us and that we were to buy our furniture in Atchison and have it sent to us. I helped him to select a very shiny dining room table, four shiny high-backed chairs, a set of dishes with a blue pattern, some easy chairs, a center table, a lamp for the parlor, and two "bedroom sets." We then bought some chenille curtains, which seemed the last word in interior decoration. Even today I never see anything resembling chenille without traveling back across the country to a tiny stone house on the shore of the Arkansas River where, when night fell of a winter's evening, we drew our gay crimson curtains and sat secure and snug while coyotes cried or blizzards raged outside on the lonely prairie.

We left Atchison in the evening. Morning found us traveling at a good rate over the plains dotted with sagebrush as far as the eye could see. The stray towns along the way looked like collections of large packing boxes set down at random. The houses, which boasted no paint, had stovepipes instead of chimneys and were roughly roofed with flapping tar paper. Each tiny railroad station was literally overshadowed by an enormous heap of white cattle bones ready for transportation to the button factories. My father told me it had been a terrible winter, one blizzard after another had swept the plains with dense clouds of snow traveling so swiftly that each small flake was like a sharp, winged dart; against these whirly weapons neither man nor beast could stand. One bitter winter's day on a railroad journey across Kansas, he said he could dimly see, as the winds angrily tore the snow clouds into shreds, half-frozen cattle leaning exhausted against the telegraph poles, while gaunt gray wolves waited at a little distance till they should drop. Range cattle perished by the thousands, and the few buffalo still left apparently succumbed, for buffalo skulls with horns attached were found along with the skulls of cattle after the snow had melted.

We arrived at our destination, the town of Kendall, in Hamilton County, about six in the evening. As we started across the prairie toward the lumberyard office, which was to be our home until the stone house was completed, something whistled past my ear causing me to jump and clutch my father's arm.

"A bullet," said he. "Don't be alarmed. The cowboys are apt to get a little gay about now, but they're capital marksmen, they won't hit you."

This explanation did not completely reassure me, and what with expecting to be shot by an erring bullet from a drunken cowboy's gun, bitten by a rattlesnake coiled beneath a sagebrush, or jumped on by a hideous tarantula, I arrived at the lumberyard in anything but a peaceful frame of mind.

The office consisted of three rooms. One room had a tall desk, several spittoons, and a pot-bellied stove. Another had a bedstead of planed boards, with wooden slats in lieu of springs on which rested a large tick stuffed with straw. The only other furniture in the room was a pile of window frames. This room had five doors but no windows. Of the two outside doors, one opened directly on the prairie, the other on a platform overlooking the lumberyard. In these doors were panes of glass that served as windows. Of the three remaining doors, one opened into the office, another into a windowless storage shed, and the third into the chamber that was to be my room until the stone house was finished. It had for furnishings a homemade bedstead without springs but with a real mattress and pillows, a homemade washstand, and one store chair. On the floor was a buffalo skin.

As soon as I had washed my face and hands at the little washstand in the corner of my room, we started for a hotel. The town of five hundred inhabitants had, my father remarked, six hotels. The one we entered had a room furnished with long tables at which were gathered, by actual count, twenty-seven cowboys in flannel shirts with trousers tucked into their boots. They were vigorously eating huge chunks of antelope steak soaked in something resembling red tomato ketchup, obtained from bottles scattered up and down the mussy white oilcloth table cover. Swarms of large flies buzzed about the room and crawled over the plates piled with warty cream-of-tartar biscuits. A few flies lay dead or dying on the black poison papers floating in white saucers with which the tables were decorated. There were two places set for us with unbreakable plates turned down. Beside each plate was an unbreakable white mug and a steel knife and fork. My father and I sat down. He reached a long arm and drew in a platter of antelope steak, a plate of biscuits, and a bottle of sauce, helped himself and me plentifully, and the meal was served. Meanwhile the cowboys, who had finished, noisily pushed back their chairs, stuck wooden toothpicks in their mouths, grabbed their slouch hats, hitched up their trousers, and strode out.

As we walked back to the lumberyard over the darkening prairie, I told my father that I thought it would be pleasanter if we could begin housekeeping at once. He readily agreed with me and we turned back to the town's one street to make a few purchases. Each store had its own boardwalk, which rested on posts raised about a foot from the ground. Along the outer edge sat the cowboys, smoking, chewing, and swapping yarns. Not a woman had I seen, excepting the huge creature in a Mother Hubbard who had several times replenished the platters of antelope meat and the plates of biscuits.

We bought, in the combination store, a teakettle, a saucepan, some tin plates, a few steel knives, forks, and spoons, and several cups and saucers. We tried to buy a dishpan, but there were none in stock, so we took a small wooden washtub, evidently a child's toy tub. This, by the way, was the only toy of any sort I ever saw in the town. It stood us in good stead as a dishpan for more than a year. We then bought, in the same store, tea, sugar, butter, milk, and other groceries.

Our next stop was at the bakery, which stood at the edge of the settlement where prairie-dog town began. The baker, Sandy McPherson, was a Scotchman, as one could tell the minute he opened his mouth. He was tall and raw-boned with the bearing of a Highlander. Such a man, I felt, should be striding over the moors with his gun on his shoulder and his dogs at his heels. No sooner had the thought occurred to me than three hounds came gamboling into the shop. While Sandy McPherson caressed them, they lapped his hands and face with their lithe tongues. Without stopping to wash his hands, he took a loaf of bread and a dozen little flat cakes from the shelf and put them into a bag which he handed to my father. One of the dogs, in the meantime, in his gamboling had managed to run afoul of a huge mixing bowl of dough and to get his forefeet embedded in the pasty mass. Sandy yanked him by the scruff of the neck and righted the mixing bowl, merely remarking that he'd make a baker of that animal yet, since this was the third batch of bread the dog had tried to knead.

The sun had set when we arrived at the lumberyard, laden with parcels. My father opened the door of the office and almost fell over our trunks which had been shoved in while we were out. After fumbling around in the dark, he found and lighted a small hand lamp, the tiny flame of which was almost eclipsed by the black smoke with which the chimney was encrusted. By its feeble ray, we deposited our purchases on shelves and took from one of the trunks bedclothes for the two beds. By the time we had made the beds it was after ten o'clock. As there was but one lamp my father lent it to me. I was too tired to lay my clothes on the chair properly, as Aunty Fox had taught me to do, and too fearful of a rattlesnake under the bed to kneel on the floor for my prayers. I dropped my clothes in a little heap on the buffalo skin, climbed into bed, put my head under the covers, and fell into a dreamless sleep.

Bright and early my father called me. For a moment I thought that I was in my little bed at number nine Elm Street, with darling Aunt Anna close by. I started to call her and, in the act, came to myself. The charming little room in my grandfather's pleasant home was nearly two thousand miles away, beyond the Arkansas, the Missouri, and the Mississippi, beyond the Great Lakes, on the shores of the Atlantic. My present room was somewhat like old white Charley's box stall. I wondered what Aunt Anna would say if she could see it. Well, the more strange things happened, the more I should have to tell her when I saw her, for I never doubted that I should see her. After all, I was having a great adventure, such an adventure as few sixteen-year-old girls born of respectable parents could have. I decided that I was a fortunate person, hoped new adventures would come thick and fast, and sprang out of bed to meet them.

My father reported that the stove had struck, presumably because the pipe was choked with soot. At any rate, its only response to his well-intentioned efforts was a dense volume of smoke that filled the office and poured from the open door so alarmingly that Grandma White, who lived in a shack behind the yard, came to see if the lumber was on fire. When the place was free of smoke, we breakfasted on milk, bread and butter, and cake.

The problem of how to get hot water for the dishes was readily solved. Grandma White, when she saw me on the platform in the rear behind the office with my tub and dishes, sent me a full tomato can of hot water by the hand of her eight-year-old grandson, who was minus a palate. He presented the can saying, "Gir here voo hok wauken," and every morning, noon, and night thereafter my appearance on the platform with my dish tub brought him to me with the can and his cheerful, "Gir here voo hok wauken."

After three weeks of such hit-and-miss housekeeping, our little stone house was finished. It had a front yard, a backyard, and two little side yards, surrounded by a neat picket fence, along which minute catalpa trees were set at regular intervals. On one side lived Mr. and Mrs. McCann and their seven children, in a sod house with tin roof made from old cans, painted vermillion. On the other side, in a two-room shack, dwelt Mayor Bell, with his wife and baby. Mrs. Bell was an efficient manager, and cloth being scarce, she had used a flour sack for one of her son's garments. While she hung out the washing, I often saw him creeping toward her, bearing on his stern the legend, "Pillsbury's Best."

Our house was on the old Santa Fe Trail, over which all day long in summertime the covered wagons, drawn by horses and oxen, lumbered past our door. Those who arrived late in the day camped about a hundred feet to the west on the "Sand Crick," the dry bed of a stream that had apparently disappeared in the earth, as water could always be found by digging a few feet below the surface. Five or six cottonwoods, the only trees for miles, bordered the crick and made a desirable stable for the draft animals, mules, horses, or oxen, when camp was made.

During the summer of 1886 I counted in one week seventy-six covered wagons passing our door, some of them bearing the time-honored legend, "Pike's Peak or Bust." Many a night I have been suddenly wakened by the coyotes' cries and have jumped out of bed to look at the white covered wagons, ghostly in the moonlight, and at the dark patches on the ground where the travelers were sleeping.

One morning in particular, I remember looking out just as the sun was rising. The sagebrush, ruffled by the morning wind, looked like a silver sea stretching away and away to the horizon. Three wagons with their canvas tops were the ships upon the sea. In the foreground was what appeared to be a pink-and-white raft. While I looked, from under the raft crawled a man fully dressed. He gathered a few bits of dried sagebrush wood and soon had a fire going in the bed of the creek. Then out came a woman, fully dressed. From the wagon she took a saucepan, which she filled with bacon scraps and placed over the fire. Finally out came a small boy in blue overalls and flannel shirt, a perfect little man. The woman then took up the raft, which turned out to be bedclothes, including a pink-and-white quilt in a pattern like the one in Aunt Mary Handy's Cape Cod cottage. The sight of these people sleeping on the ground, and sitting around the brushwood fire while they drank coffee and ate bacon and a substance that resembled ship biscuit, somewhat removed my fear of poisonous snakes and insects.

Our town was supposed to be on the trail that Coronado followed in his search for the seven cities of Cibola.[5] Therefore, the first settlers who camped on the site gave it a Spanish name, Zamora. Later on this was changed to Fort Aubrey, Aubrey being the name of an army officer who, at the time of Indian massacres, made a sort of marathon dash on horseback that ended at Zamora. When the railroad was put through and a section house was built, an enterprising settler by the name of Kendall decided to rename the town after himself. There being no objection, the settlement was duly divorced from its old names and dubbed Kendall, which is the name it still bears.

On the opposite shore of the Arkansas River were the sand hills of the so-called American Desert, great inland dunes, treeless, flowerless, and uninhabited save by birds of prey, noisome reptiles, wolves, and coyotes. In the daytime one could count on seeing either a yellow-and-brown rattlesnake sunning itself on the top of a dune, a hairy red tarantula scurrying into its hole, or a slithering centipede, less dangerous to meet, but more unsightly than the other two. From these hills at night came the long-drawn baying of wolves, the mournful cries of the coyotes, and the eerie hooting of the prairie owls. I never went on foot into the sand hills, but rode my calico Texas horse, a raw-boned beast who was as dependable as a saddle horse, but resented being hitched to the buggy, when he sometimes stood on his hind legs, sometimes balked, or again ran at full speed with the buggy leaping like a wild thing in his wake.

The town lay in the river bottoms at the foot of a bluff, the beginning of the "high prairie," which was covered with a thick mat of short, curly buffalo grass, sprinkled with many colored flowers. Most conspicuous were the white bell-shaped blossoms of the yucca which, surrounded by swordlike leaves, sometimes attained a height of four or five feet. This plant was known as soap weed, the legend being that the Indian women used to cut blocks of its root for scrubbing purposes. The purple flowers of the loco, which "locoed" (intoxicated) cattle, the small dark red blossoms of the Indian bread root, the white and purple lupines, and the yellow and magenta flowers of the cactus made of the prairie a veritable magic carpet over which it was my great joy to gallop my calico horse.

My father had to make frequent trips to New Mexico, and during his absence a certain May Mattress, from a ranch just beyond the town, stayed with me. On one of these occasions the cowboys came in on a round-up and "shot up the town," which meant that for hours after night had fallen they were shooting into the air—*bang, bang*—shouting in unison as they shot, "Damn, damn."

One night, after an unusually wild shooting bout, I had fallen asleep only to be rudely wakened by a handful of pebbles thrown against the window near my bed. At last, I thought, the cowboys had discovered that we two women were alone. More pebbles came in a rattling shower. I reached under my pillow for the loaded bulldog revolver my father had given me as a protector and crept quickly to a point from which I could see without being seen. Bing, bing, bing, bing, more pebbles hit the window. I could make out the shadow of the pump and, to my horror, I saw beside it the moving shadow of a man in a broad-brimmed hat. Soon the man himself came into view. I followed him with my eyes as he stopped to pick up another handful of pebbles. As he rose and turned his face toward the window, I recognized him and shouted, "Father!"

"Please let me in," he said. "I've been throwing pebbles at your window for some time as I did not want to frighten you by shouting."

He had come home because of an important election about to take place. Kendall was in the very center of Hamilton County and was striving for the county seat. Two other towns contested for the honor. As it turned out, one of these towns pulled wires so successfully that by legislative act the county was cut in half and poor Kendall, being in the exact center, was divided into two parts, one part being in Hamilton, the other in Kearney County. The population, stranded beside the county line, dwindled to a mere handful, and many pioneer projectors, my father and uncle among the number, were ruined. The unfortunate slicing of Kendall was not the sole cause of my uncle's failure, but was a contributing factor to the general collapse of the building boom.

My father was obliged to remain to wind up the lumber and real estate business to which he was committed. Morning, noon, and a good part of the night he labored to save what he could from the wreckage of his ventures. I saw little of him excepting at mealtime, when he silently bolted his food and rushed back to the lumberyard.

As for myself, I entered upon various activities with vigor and enthusiasm. First, I helped May who, upon my father's return from New Mexico, had remained to do the housework. She was a stolid creature, as placid as a pet cow, as unimaginative as a hen, as lacking in human interest as a codfish. After dishes were wiped and beds made, I pressed flowers, made crude water-color sketches of covered wagons and prairie scenes, searched for agates and carnelians, to be found in little islands of pebbles which looked as if they had been deposited by a rapidly receding tide, and visited the neighboring quarries where a petrified fish, perfect in form, had been found. As for shells, the rock was filled with them; they could be seen in almost every block of the stone with which our house was built. Then there was the garden, as unpromising a piece of earth for cultivation as could be found. A hoe made no impression upon it, and I was compelled to get upon my knees and prepare it for seeding with an ax. After many varieties of seeds had been planted, I sedulously watered the ground, pumping the water and carrying great pails with difficulty from the pump to the garden. By these strenuous methods I succeeded in raising one row of multicolored four-o'clocks, which I loved even as the Count de Charney loved his picciola;[6] and my garden of prairie memories is hedged with bush four o'clocks covered with red, yellow, white, and striped blossoms.

I had practically no companions and I longed to become acquainted with a girl about my own age who brought our milk from her father's ranch several miles out on the high prairie. She came to our house about five in the morning, an hour when I was usually asleep. One afternoon, when she was in town on an errand, she stopped at the fence to speak to me while I was in the act of worshiping my four-o'clocks.

"Ain't they beautiful!" she exclaimed.

"I'll save some of the seeds for you," I replied.

"Oh, will you?" she said. "I'd admire to have them." Then she continued, "Father and the other men came in with a lot of horses yesterday. If you'll be up when I come tomorrow, you can ride back with me and see them."

I promised, and she rode away sitting astride her broad-backed horse.

I did not consult my father about this visit. He had not taken me into his confidence since the unfortunate slicing of the county. There were times when it was best not to take him into mine. I had made up my mind that it would be a good thing to see the cowgirl's ranch and I wished nothing to interfere with the plan. She wakened me by the same pebble-throwing method my father had employed, and at 5:20 we were on our way in the democrat wagon used for delivering milk. At the ranch house, a large one-room dugout with mud walls and floor, I had a glass of milk and several cream-of-tartar biscuits, and then went with the cowgirl to drive the cows to pasture. I rode a mule with no saddle. I recall that his back was hard as iron, that he swished his tail violently, and that as a result of his racking gait, I felt as if I were being dragged over piles of rock. The herding completed, we went to see the horses.

In those days it was the custom to go on a marauding expedition from

Kansas into Texas perhaps twice a year to round up any unbranded ponies that had escaped from the herds and were running wild on the ranges. Among the lot were some very alluring young horses.

Said the cowgirl, "Let's pick out a coupla er good ones and ride 'em."

This she proceeded to do, and having saddled them with men's saddles, we mounted and were off. I had taken with me some crocheting consisting of a bright ball of scarlet Germantown wool, a large ivory hook, and a partially crocheted bedroom slipper. Being very proud of this crochet work, I carried it with me everywhere, and in the present instance it was tied to the horn of the saddle.

The horses loped easily, their hoofs pounding the hard alkaline earth overlaid with a sun-baked carpet of buffalo grass, spattered with flowers; the sun was about three hours up in the hard blue cloudless sky; not a tree was in sight; not the slightest rise broke the dead level of the limitless prairie.

"We'll ride till noon," said the cowgirl, "then we'll stop for a cup of coffee and a bite of bread at the McLellan's dugout. I know the trail so you need have no fear of getting lost."

At the end of the hour she said, "Suppose we run."

I had never ridden a running horse, and as he began to go faster and faster, I was prepared to cling for dear life; but the faster he ran, the more easily I sat. Indeed, the horse and I seemed motionless while the sky rushed by above us and the earth raced backward under our feet. It was glorious. Then, before I could catch it, my precious ball of scarlet wool unwound itself and fell. I tried to check my horse, and such was his response to my wish that soon he fell into a lope, then he allowed himself to be turned back till we came to the exact spot where my scarlet ball and the raveled bedroom slipper lay. I stopped him, slid down, regained my wool, and then began to consider how I was to mount my tall steed— unless he knelt like an elephant or a camel. Time after time I tried to scramble up his back. He stood quite still, only turning his head occasionally to look at me in a humorous and tolerant manner. After some twenty futile attempts, I made one more tremendous effort, and my horse and I were one again. The cowgirl, who was ahead, had not missed me at first and came loping back just as I regained the saddle.

By noon the heat was intense. My mouth was parched and my tongue felt twice its ordinary size.

"Are we almost there?" I asked.

"Pretty near," replied my companion.

At that moment I saw in the far distance a lovely lake fringed by tall trees.

"A surprise," I cried, "I didn't know there was any water on this prairie. Is the house we are going to on the lake?"

My comrade laughed. "That's a mirage," she said.

Even as she spoke, it slowly faded away leaving only the sunburned prairie and the "inverted bowl" of hard blue sky.

We rode on in silence. As we drew near the McLellan's dugout the cowgirl explained that Mrs. McLellan had come from back east and that her forebears had been Pilgrim Fathers, which fact perhaps accounted for her pioneer spirit. Because she had always had a garden in New England, she must have a garden on the prairie. Fifty sunflowers to the right, and fifty sunflowers to the left, in straight lines forming a six-foot path, marked the approach to the dugout which, like an earthworm, appeared to be crawling out of the ground. Beside it stood a molasses hogshead, which served as the well. Once a week this barrel was dragged to the river some ten miles distant and filled. It was supposed to last for a week. Thirsty as I was, the sight of the cloudy water, on which dead insects were floating, did not tempt me.

As we entered the dugout, we heard low moans. At first in the semidark cellar, we could see nothing. Then gradually the sense of blindness lifted and we saw in the far corner a woman lying on a cot. She was dressed in a faded blue Mother Hubbard, her hands were clutching the gown, and her face was white like the yucca flowers, excepting for black circles beneath her closed eyelids. As we tiptoed toward the cot, she opened her eyes and in them was a mortal fear.

"I am very ill," she breathed. "My husband has gone to Kendall for ice. I am burning, burning inside."

Then she closed her eyes and fell to moaning again, turning her head from side to side to avoid the swarming flies. I picked up a palm leaf fan which lay on the floor by the cot, and began to fan her. The cowgirl prowled about the hut and produced from the back of the stove a pot of lukewarm coffee. On a shelf nearby were some hard cream-of-tartar biscuits. Then she took my place with the fan and I forced myself to drink the dark molasseslike coffee and eat half of a bright yellow biscuit. The sick woman moaned unceasingly; the buzzing of the flies and the ticking of the clock were the only other sounds until late in the afternoon when the thud, thud of galloping hoofs was heard and Mr. McLellan staggered into the dugout with a gunnysack filled with sawdust and one precious piece of ice. The sick woman opened her eyes and murmured, "Dear John." In an instant he was kneeling beside her, putting bits of ice into her parched mouth. Soon she fell into an uneasy slumber, and seeing that there was nothing we could do, we sorrowfully mounted our horses and rode away.

"Where did he get that ice?" I questioned.

"Must have flagged the train for it," said the cowgirl.

The heat shimmered over the prairie in visible waves. Far off, we saw smoke and the red glow of a prairie fire; between us and the smoke raced a herd of graceful antelope. As the sun neared the horizon a light breeze sprang up and the sky became overcast with threatening clouds. Soon a drop of rain splashed heavily on my hand. Then, without other warning, the sky turned a purplish slate color and the rain fell in blinding curtains; thunder, such as I had never heard before, rattled and crashed unceasingly. We were not in darkness as sheets of lightning converted the prairie into a veritable witches' trysting place, with its baleful, ghostly glare.

The horses, their heads down, plodded on. We poor drenched children, blinded by the vivid flashes of lightning, deafened by the big guns of the thunder, and saddened by the thought of the two alone in the storm in their mud-walled hutch, resigned all leadership to the horses.

After what seemed years of time to my tired senses, the storm ceased as suddenly as it had come, the clouds were swept from the dark blue carpet of the night sky, and the moon poured upon the steaming prairie, a clear flood of silver light. A short half hour later we arrived at the cowgirl's ranch. When she saw the home buildings, she straightened up and said in a hoarse whisper, "Take you home first."

She left me at my own gate and loped off with the bridle of the horse I had ridden over her arm. She was a magnificent rider and one of the best sports I ever met.

Through the uncurtained window of the kitchen door, I saw my father pacing up and down. For a moment I hesitated, then I opened the door. The look of gladness that brushed the sternness and sadness from his face was like the moonlight after the storm. He quickly suppressed it, however, and without asking me where I had been, he said, "Two weeks from today you will go back East to boarding school. Now get off your wet things and go to bed." I went!

The next morning at breakfast I told my father everything. His only comment was, "You might have chosen a cooler day; our thermometer registered one hundred and twelve in the shade before noon." Later in the day he brought word that Mrs. McLellan had died and that she was to be buried in the Kendall burying ground the next day. May and I were to go to the service at the grave as he would be out of town.

On the afternoon of the funeral, lumberyard Dick harnessed my calico to the buggy, and May, the cowgirl, and I started for the graveyard on the edge of the high prairie. To reach it, we zigzagged up the face of the bluff, which divided the high prairie from the river-bottom lands.

The cowgirl told us that the McLellans had been among the first settlers of Kendall, that Mr. McLellan had been a journalist back East and had started a newspaper when he first came to Kendall, using his entire capital for the presses, type, paper stock, and other necessary supplies. He had failed and had been obliged to close his printing plant. Not having the price of the railway fare home, and being too proud to call on their folks, they had chosen to wrest a meager living from the alkaline soil of a claim.

When we reached the burial hill we found about forty vehicles of many types, from a carryall to a buckboard, drawn up in a circle. Around the space given over to mounds of earth, marked by wooden slabs lettered with the names of the dead, and within the enclosure stood a crowd of people—cowboys, gaunt women in Mother Hubbards, tow-headed children, and a few of the town officials, who wore baggy sack suits, shiny collars, and large four-in-hand neckties. The coffin, covered with prairie flowers, stood at the edge of the pit into which it would soon be lowered. Beside it stood McLellan, shaking like a child as the clergyman read the burial service. I glanced at the grave mounds and was surprised to see in the side of each a sort of excavation. I looked at the cowgirl, who whispered behind her hand, "Wolves."

As the bearers started to lower the coffin into its pit, McLellan fell upon it in a faint. After gentle hands had lifted him and laid him on the floor of one of the farm wagons, the procession of conveyances moved slowly down the bluff.

The day for my journey back East arrived. My father had allowed me to choose whether I should go to Dana Hall in Wellesley, Massachusetts, where Miss Marjorie J. Summers was then a teacher of English, or to the Vermont Methodist Seminary and Female College at Montpelier, where one of the instructors was a Miss Theodosia P. Hunt, who had been my first teacher at the little district school on the Cape. When she left at the close of her first term, she had presented me with a copy of *Lucile*,[7] with gilt-edged leaves and padded covers. On the flyleaf she had written my name, followed by the lines, "With the esteem and regard of her teacher." That inscription had won her my worshipful fealty. Who at the age of twelve could have received a more grown-up sentiment? I chose to attend the Vermont Methodist Seminary and Female College, because of the presence there of my beloved teacher.

My father saw me aboard the train, won from me a promise to write to him every Sunday, and ran to get off after the train was in motion. He jumped in the wrong direction, and my last glimpse of him was far from heartening as he literally landed on his head, and as long as I could see lay prone on the platform with men running toward him from all directions. It was several days after my arrival at Atchison, where I was to be outfitted, before I heard that he was all right, having been merely stunned.

For two weeks there was a wild orgy of sewing at Uncle Sam's house. Aunt Emma and the girls were determined that I should be a credit to the family as far as clothes had anything to do with the matter, and no pains were spared to have my wardrobe complete.

Aunt Emma's last words to me were, "Edith, you have a long journey before you. If any woman tries to speak to you, answer her politely, but do not go anywhere with her." This caution arose from the fact that it was an open custom in the Midwest for women of questionable character to meet every train, to waylay any unprotected girl, and to lure her to some infamous house from which escape was difficult.

My father had written to Miss Hunt, who had kindly invited me to spend Sunday at her home in Enfield, Massachusetts, and to go on with her to Montpelier the next day. Unfortunately my train was several hours late, and I arrived at Springfield, Massachusetts, where I was to change trains, at seven o'clock on a Saturday evening, after the last Enfield train had left.

"There will be no train till Monday," the ticket agent told me.

As I left the ticket window a plainly dressed, sweet-faced woman came to me and said, "I heard you inquiring for a ticket to Enfield. Have you no friends in Springfield?"

To say I was frightened is putting it mildly; I could not have been more terrified had a rattlesnake sounded his rattle at my very feet. I faltered that I must get to Enfield that night.

Said the woman, "I am a YWCA worker, and you could stay at the YW tonight and hire someone to drive you over tomorrow."

Said I, recoiling from this ingratiating serpent in human disguise, "No, I must go tonight."

"Well, then, I must see what I can do to help you," she replied, and off she went to the ticket window.

Cold with apprehension, I considered what my next move should be. Should I telegraph Aunt Emma in Atchison for advice, should I take refuge in the streets, or should I call the police for protection? Almost sixty-five years have passed since the incident, yet few of my memories are clearer or more detailed.

From the ticket window the yw worker returned to me and said, "I find there is a train for Bondsville, a town only a few miles from Enfield, at ten o'clock tonight. I will come back at that time and ask the conductor to look after you."

Now the conductor was a man, and I had not been warned against men. I thanked her heartily, and choosing the lightest part of the station in which to pass the two-and-one-half hours, I sat down, clutching my traveling bag with one hand and my umbrella with the other. When at a quarter before ten she arrived, I had no longer any doubt of her good intentions. In the few remaining minutes I told her where I had come from and where I was going. I was rather surprised that she did not know Miss Hunt, whom I felt should be widely known as a teacher at the Methodist Seminary and Female College.

The conductor, a burly, bearded individual, spoke to me kindly as we steamed off. Besides myself in the car, there were perhaps a dozen laborers in overalls. When we arrived at Bondsville, the end of the line, the conductor escorted me to the waiting room, which was occupied by several intoxicated men who were having a noisy argument. I was, therefore, allowed to sit in the ticket office while the conductor and the station agent cleared out the waiting room. A few minutes later my friend, the conductor, with his lantern hooked over his left arm, took me on his right arm and led forth into the starless night, across the tracks, and along what felt like a very dusty road. There were few lighted windows in the houses we passed, and even the boardinghouse into which he took me was indifferently illuminated by one depot lamp above a counter, which appeared to be also a bar. I had never been in so dingy and dirty a place before. The Kendall hotels had been far from clean, but their dirt was not over a year old. This dirt was hoary with antiquity, and there was no attempt at concealment.

I thanked my kind conductor for his courteous attentions to one whom he had never seen before and in all likelihood would never see again. Then I wrote my name in a fly-specked register and was shown to my room by an untidy clerk in shirtsleeves.

When I had made sure that the door was locked, I looked about by the dim light of a small hand lamp with blackened chimney. The sheets and pillowcases had evidently been slept on many times, the towels on the rack were dingy, and the cake of yellow soap was black with grime. I spread my coat over the pillow, lay down without removing my clothes, and fell asleep as readily as though I had been in the little white bed in my New Bedford room.

I woke with the sun shining in my face and sprang up ready for the next adventure. Life was certainly exciting, but it was also safe if one trusted in the good God and kept one's head. I combed my hair, dipped a clean handkerchief into the water pitcher, wiped my face and hands, unlocked the door, went down to the desk, and asked for transportation to Enfield. In a few minutes I was on my way with a driver who seemed a trifle too familiar. I tried, therefore, to appear twenty-six instead of sixteen, with apparent success for he soon ceased to question me and drove along in moody silence.

Miss Hunt had not changed, and she and her aged father and mother seemed to consider me a great traveler and must needs hear of all my adventures.

On Monday afternoon we arrived at Montpelier and were driven up a steep hill crowned with the buildings of the school. The dormitories looked to me like the tenements in the New Bedford mill district—long, many-windowed, yellow-painted houses, with as much architectural style as a Noah's Ark house. The red brick edifice in which classes were held stood at one side of a scrubby campus. It was equipped with a bell tower and, like the dormitories, was uncompromisingly plain. However, if the appearance of these buildings tended to be depressing, the view was sufficiently inspiring to make me feel that it was good to be there. Beyond the valley, in which nestled the beautiful little town of Montpelier, rose tier upon tier of forest-clad hills, and above all, majestic against the sky, towered the purple heights of Camel's Hump. As my eyes rested on this splendid panorama, I forgot the ugly buildings on the scrubby campus and realized that I had but to "lift up my eyes unto the hills" in time of need. With a last long look at the encircling mountains, I turned and entered the bleak dormitory that was to be my home for four of the pleasantest years of my life.

Miss Hunt took me to her room on the first floor, and when I had removed my hat and coat, she conducted me to the preceptress, a sweet-faced young person, who was a recent graduate of the seminary. In her office I was assigned a room on the second floor and given my room-mate's name, Rena Lane. Miss Hunt went upstairs with me to my room, where I found Rena and a certain Miss Purrington, who was busily running a sewing machine. Rena was a pale, sickly looking girl, but she seemed radiantly happy. A little later Miss Hunt told me that the poor girl, who was a penniless orphan, had been for years a worker in the Lowell textile mills, that she had been sick almost unto death, and that Miss Purrington, a teacher in the evening school which she attended had raised a fund for her education, and here she was. Her friend was at present making simple dresses and underclothing so that her protégée's half of the clothes closet and bureau drawers would be well stocked.

For the first term this exemplary girl was a model for me. I had never imagined that anyone could be so eager for learning and could possess such a capacity for absorbing it. Unfortunately her joy was short-lived, for when the cold autumn winds began to blow, she was stricken with her old complaint. Then did Miss Hunt's loving kindness shine as the sun. She took the girl into her own room, which was warmer than ours, and cared for her tenderly until it was all too apparent that death waited at the door. Her old friend, the teacher, was summoned and came to take her back to Lowell where some relatives had agreed to care for her. She parted from us with a smile, remarking that God had been good to give her so happy a time with such kind friends.

The house in which we roomed was three stories high, in a shape like the letter *E*. In the first long bar lived the girls, in the short bar was the dining room, in the third long bar lived the boys, and across the front were the rooms of the preceptress and the principal as well as the reception room.

The bedrooms were carpeted with ingrain carpet of a red-and-brown pattern, and each was furnished with a wide bedstead, a study table, bureau, washstand, several chairs, and a stove. Our stove was named "Cushion," as I well remember because I once stumbled and sat on this iron cushion when the fire was going.

In the early fall and the late spring, these rooms were delightful places of abode. From October to May they were lethal chambers. The only heat was furnished by the stoves, one in each room. Our Cushion, a mere oblong iron box on legs, had sides made to resemble the type of upholstery which runs to buttons. It was my custom, on going to class, to fill Cushion to the top with wood and to leave the draft and the damper partly open. On my return from class, the room might have a temperature of eighty degrees, or again it might have a temperature of forty degrees.

Before getting into bed at night, I laid beside Cushion a newspaper, a dustpan of kindling, and many sticks of wood. It was not an enjoyable feat, that of stepping from a warm bed into a temperature often far below freezing to kindle a fire by which to dress. Then there was the long walk through totally unheated corridors to the dining room. With others, I waited on table and so paid for part of my tuition. There were certain liquid and solid foods that each waitress had to place on the table before the meal was served. The formula, which for four years I repeated in the morning, was "bread, doughnuts, milk"; at noon, it was "butter, water, pie." This bears testimony to the fact that two good old New England standbys, doughnuts and pie, were not lacking from the bill of fare.

At 8:30 A.M. the entire company of boys and girls attended chapel exercises. What with changing from overheated rooms to icy corridors, from stuffy, ill-ventilated classrooms to the stormswept campus, often minus rubbers and hats, ten to twenty boys and girls were frequently in bed with severe colds. Those who survived four winters at the good old school might, indeed, consider themselves hardened soldiers. I use the word *soldiers* advisedly, as the dormitories had been barracks during the Civil War. Many of the survivors came off with battle scars. I, myself, confess to weakness in the arms, which I attribute to my daily duty of carrying huge graniteware dishes, with food for eight persons, from the kitchen to the dining room—a heavy burden for a person who tipped the scales at ninety-two pounds.

Three or four times a day I went to class. I remember studying Latin, Greek, and French, astronomy, botany, algebra, and geometry. As for history, literature, and the English language, they were, as far as I can recall, quite left out of my curriculum.

The classrooms were furnished with hard wooden settees, and the walls were lined with blackboards. The chapel, a barnlike room also furnished with long yellow settees, had a rostrum with a small pulpit, at which our principal read the Scriptures and led us in prayer. Occasionally some good Methodist of high repute spoke to us of the missionary fields in China, Africa, or the South Sea Islands, and once a very great person who was going to present the school with the munificent sum of one thousand dollars told us how fortunate we were to be students at a school as fine as the Vermont Methodist Seminary and Female College. We felt very important and applauded him to the echo.

At four o'clock, when classes were over for the day, I swung my strap of books under the table in my room and entered wholeheartedly into the business of living. In the autumn we played baseball vigorously; in the winter we skated on the flooded campus or tobogganed in the fields that sloped down from the hill on all sides; in the spring we played tennis or walked in the woods behind the dormitories.

At half past five, I was due in the dining room to do my share of table setting. After supper it was a rule, the penalty for breaking it being expulsion, that each girl should study in her own room till half past nine, when she was allowed a half hour of freedom. At half past ten all lights were to be out.

To brighten the period from half past seven to half past nine, I went at intervals to the window and tried to see what my neighbors, the "self-boarders," were doing in their house, which was opposite our windows and about fifty feet distant. For those students who could not afford to live in the school boardinghouse, there were two rooming houses, one for boys and one for girls, called self-boarding houses. The rooms in these houses had only the bare essentials in furnishings. Two self-boarders would eat, sleep, bathe, wash and iron, keep their provisions, and cook, in one small room. The privations they endured in their quest for education rendered them truly appreciative of the crumbs of knowledge that they eagerly gathered; and their conversation convinced me that they really got something worthwhile from the Greek and Latin and other stuff, which I so sincerely hated. An invincible courage with which they met and conquered the conditions their poverty imposed, an immense hunger for knowledge as set forth in the books, and a simple faith in God as a real and ever-present help, characterized both boys and girls and gave me an abiding affection for Vermont as represented by these earnest young folk.

The two great events of the year were the fall trip to Camel's Hump to see the painted leaves on a thousand hills and the early spring party in the sugar bush. We were given an entire day for each of these events. My memory of the spring holiday is especially vivid. The maple grove where sugaring-off was in process was miles from the school, and we went to it in pungs with straw on the floor and long boards for seats on either side. Right into the woods we drove to the slab-sided sugar house, where we deposited our lunch boxes and watched the sap boiling in great vats and sending forth clouds of fragrant steam.

Then for an hour we prowled through the woods, walking easily on the hard crust of the snow and sampling the sap, which was slowly filling hundreds of buckets hanging on the tree trunks. When luncheon time came we found that the boys had shoveled a clear space in the snow and had made a fire of dry wood. Over this they had erected a tripod from which hung an old iron kettle half-filled with merrily boiling sap. The boxes of luncheon were fetched from the sugar house and we sat down on logs that the boys had placed in lieu of benches.

I soon found there was a regular form of procedure. First, each member of the party took an uncooked egg from her lunch box and passed it to the boy who had charge of the kettle. One by one he dropped the eggs gently into the boiling syrup. While waiting for them to become hard, we ate thick sandwiches of bread and butter and mammoth doughnuts. The trick with the cooked eggs consisted of removing the edible portions so carefully that as much as possible of the eggshell was left intact. This formed a cup that was then filled with boiling syrup and set in the snow where it soon hardened. When the shell was chipped off, there remained a luscious cake of perfectly fresh maple sugar. In the lunch boxes were large tin spoons, and with these we dipped up spoonfuls of boiling sap that we poured on the snow crust where it waxed into thin cakes called "sheep skins." When one had eaten sheep skins to repletion, one ate a vinegar pickle and began again on sugar.

In the early afternoon, after we had walked and romped in the woods till we were happily tired, we climbed into the pungs and were whisked along over the glistening snow by broad-backed, tireless, plow horses. The thought of many lessons to be learned in the bleak hours between seven-thirty and nine-thirty that evening never entered our heads, and we arrived at the campus with restored vigor, glowing with health, and shouting like a conquering army.

During the winter and spring vacations I either remained at the school or visited one or another of my schoolmates, who were all very generous with their invitations. My first winter vacation was spent with Flora Corwin in Chelsea, Vermont, a lovely little village that lay in a mountain valley, eighteen miles from a railroad station. We went by stagecoach up and up into the mountains as far as we could go on wheels; then we stopped at a sort of wayside inn and changed to runners. It was very cold, and the driver brought us hot soapstones for our feet. For the next nine miles, we rode among the snowclad hills, their whiteness pricked by pointed firs from whose branches much of the snow had fallen. There were few dwellings, and the loneliness seemed to me even greater than that of the prairie. About half past nine, far below us appeared the twinkling lights of the village. The horses, as eager as the humans to be at the end of their journey, trotted down the hill at a great pace, entered the main street of Chelsea with merry jingling of bells, and stopped before the comfortable colonial house in which Flora lived. There for the next few weeks we lived on the fat of the land and forgot that there were such trials as the conjugation of Latin verbs and the solving of algebraic problems.

One of my spring vacations was passed with a schoolmate whose father had a sawmill on a little stream that ran singing through a beech wood, where the ground was hidden by a carpet of maidenhair ferns woven into delightful patterns that changed with every breath of the wind. In those woods grew so many varieties of violets that I dare not give the number I seem to remember. There were deep purple violets with long stems; there were large and small blue, white, yellow, and lavender violets; and there were violets called pansies. Among the other flowers I recall hepaticas, twin flowers, bloodroot, trillium, and claytonia. These flowers differed as to fragility of texture and delicacy of color from the flowers of the plains as the Puritan maidens of Plymouth differed from the gaily decked Indian girls of the southwestern mesas.

My first summer vacation I spent in Cambridge, Massachusetts, with the aunt whom in childhood I had met in Pepperell at the little farm near the "Pinnacle." Unable to wrest a living from the stony fields, she had gone to Cambridge with her sick husband, who could do little for the support of his wife and child, and had taken a position in the mailing department of the Riverside Press. In addition to this piece of work, she ran, with the help of a friend whose acquaintance she had made in Pepperell, a successful boardinghouse. Her heart was as large as her means were limited. She at once made me feel at home and manifested an interest in my welfare by making me several dresses, my Kansas outfits being so worn out that I was barely presentable.

Hearing me say that I longed for a tennis set, my aunt got me an opportunity to read copy at the press for several weeks. What a thrill I felt when early one morning I entered the place where books were made, inhaled the oily odor, and heard the thump of the mighty presses. At half past eight the manuscript of a book was put into my hands and I

Edith Guerrier (lower left) *as a member of "The Tennis Club," at the Vermont Methodist Seminary and Female College, Montpelier. Reproduced courtesy of the Whaling Museum, New Bedford, Massachusetts.*

began to read it to the proofreader. It was a great moment! Thenceforth the weeks went quickly and happily till the copy reader, whose place I had taken, returned, and the contents of my pay envelopes were sufficient for the purchase of a tennis set. The four rackets, the net, and balls made a sizable package, but I refused to be parted from it and carried it with me from Cambridge to Montpelier.

Another summer vacation I spent at Wellesley, Massachusetts, in the smallest house I have ever seen. One tiny space on the ground floor served as living room, dining room, and kitchen. From this room a diminutive stairway led to an attic, which was divided into two small chambers. The bedsteads were under the eaves, and on a hot summer evening a small window admitted just sufficient air to keep one from stifling. My father, who had come on from Kansas, leased this toy cottage for the period of my summer vacation. In order that my time might be well spent, he sent me to a summer school of languages at Wellesley Hills, where I studied French. Not having the slightest gift for acquiring any foreign language, I was as great "a thorn in the flesh" of my teacher as she was in mine.

My days were well occupied. I rose at six and prepared breakfast, which we ate hastily; then I cleared the table, washed the dishes, and walked to Wellesley Hills where, until noon, I stewed in the sour juices of French grammar and conversed in a language understood by no one, least of all by myself, then walked back. As soon as I entered the house I began to prepare dinner. After the dishes were done I swept and dusted the tiny house and for the rest of the afternoon murdered the French language with the aid of pencil and paper. I think my father must have considered that the studying of this language would have a refining influence upon me, for whatever studies I pursued, he always specified that the French language should be one of them. It occurs to me, as I write these lines, that it may have been because of our French ancestry, and because of our name, which according to the family legend was given by a French king to a distant ancestor for prowess on the battlefield.

My father read much and wrote verses. He loved nature and was never as happy as when he was sauntering through the woods or meadows, far from human habitation. Had he been provided with a comfortable income from a principal so securely tied that the process of untying it would have daunted him, he could have followed the lead of his tastes and would have been considered a charming and unique personality.

Forced as he was to do work in which he had no interest, he was like the caged squirrel on his little wheel, who keeps it going because he must do something, but the faster he makes it go the more he longs for freedom. At the end of the summer my father's purse was empty, that is, empty except for the sum put aside for my education. The emptiness of his purse only worried him as it affected my prospects in life.

My four happy years at Montpelier came to an end all too soon, sooner it seemed than the class poem I was commissioned to write. It took me weeks to get the thing going and then it took me as many weeks to stop it. It was a heroic effort, but finally even my father was convinced that one whose only sense of poetry was the matching of the last syllable of every other line lacked poetic fire, divine or otherwise.

As I glance back at my writings, I seem to have produced much on the pleasure of vacations and little on the business of getting an education. As a matter of fact, I felt that the lessons in the books had nothing to do with the actual business of living. I read words, words, words; I committed to memory words, words, words; and I forgot words, words, words. It was not the fault of my teachers, but of my upbringing that vacations and holidays, tennis and skating, and roaming in fairy woods meant more, a thousandfold more, than classroom periods.

THREE

A Single Woman,

1891–1917

 The year I graduated, my father came out of the West for good. As the Kansas boom had swept the state and disappeared, leaving nothing but a trail of ruin to mark its meteoric passage, he was constrained to start again, for the ninth or tenth time, at the bottom of the ladder, as a bookkeeper in Brockton, Massachusetts.

On leaving the Seminary, I went to the house where my father boarded with hospitable and kindly people who readily made me feel like one of the family, even to the extent of allowing me to share a room with one of the daughters who was my own age.

With the first few dollars my father accumulated, he had bought a lot in Campello, a suburb of Brockton, then for the most part an undeveloped tract of uninteresting country overgrown with small pines. We were both very proud to be the owners of a piece of land, as our Pepperell farm, excepting a small woodlot, had been sold to pay my school bills. The first Sunday I spent in Brockton we went to our lot and sat down beside a small pine to consider what was to be done with me.

My father, ever optimistic, said, "As soon as I can put up a little house on this lot, we can manage very nicely on my salary"—twenty-seven dollars a week, I think it was. "In the meantime, have you made up your mind what you would like to do?"

"I should like to be an artist," I said.

"Have you any special talent in that direction?" asked my father.

"Not that I know of," I said, "still that's what I want to be."

We sat long among the scrubby little pine trees discussing ways and means, with the result that I was provided with sketching blocks, paints, and brushes and was sent to a farmhouse at Brewster, on Cape Cod, for the summer. It was a foregone conclusion that if I had talent I should produce beautiful pictures.

That summer I began to notice for the first time that my father appeared to be growing old. His hardships, his army experience, the death of my mother, his western failure, and above all the fact that he had progressed no further than to a clerk's stool had silvered his hair and written lines on his forehead. I felt that I must no longer be a burden to him. I had an idea that I could produce little Christmas card drawings that would sell. Therefore, rain or shine, I rose early and worked from dawn till dark. Perhaps the sketches were not so bad. While they were not salable, they had sufficient interest to convince my father that I had the makings of an artist. Without consulting me, he sold our precious Campello lot with its hardy scrub pine forest, and with some of the money started me on my career at the Museum School of Art in Boston.[1]

I had a room at the Berkeley Street Annex of the Young Women's Christian Association. It was about ten feet long and six feet wide. One window opened upon the street; the other gave light to the bathroom. This was not a very tight window and served to some extent as a ventilator for the bathroom. In order to reach my room, I passed through another room occupied by three persons, cheerful souls, who always gave me a kindly greeting. For this accommodation, including three meals a day and some laundry, I pair four dollars and twenty-five cents a week. I had a roof over my head and sufficient food.

The first morning that I passed the manager of the dining room, I said innocently, "Good morning!"—two words.

She replied in four times that number, "I have no time to say, 'Good morning.'"

In 1891 the activities of the Museum School of Art were scattered about the old rococo red brick building, which stood where the Hotel Copley Plaza now stands. We set up our easels first in the bust room and when we were, as the boys said, sufficiently "busted," we rose to the attic and there, under the leads in the unfinished upper part of the building, we drew from life. In the basement room were classes in design, and in a little brick building in the rear were the portrait classes.

I drew badly. Mr. Frank W. Benson, the eminent American painter, then our instructor, with patient aloofness strengthened my wavering outlines and permitted himself to remark, day after day, "Draw what you see, not what you think you know." Mr. Anson K. Gross, who instructed us in perspective, impressed upon me the dictum both philosophical and technical that however the lines of endeavor might appear to reach a point, that point on near approach always vanished into an undistinguishable distance. Dr. Edward Emerson, the son of Ralph Waldo Emerson, taught artistic anatomy. He always stood beside a beautiful skeleton and handled the dry "bons," as he called them, with such enthusiastic vigor that small finger and toe bones were frequently jerked across the room. I went through the first year in a foggy way, never quite sure of myself. My efforts were as unsatisfactory to me as they were to my patient instructors. I began to be afraid I had no gift worth the blind effort I was putting forth.

Once a month I spent Sunday with my father in Brockton. Though he was not yet sixty, he had become an old man, bent and sorrowful. I had come to feel toward him more like a mother than a daughter, and longed to have for him a comfortable home in which there would be a study with many books and an open fireplace. He would not hear of my giving up the art school, so the second year, without consulting him, I set about finding some work. I had earned money at the Riverside Press by reading copy and at the Montpelier school by waiting on table. The former meant a full-time job; the latter, only a few hours a day. I therefore applied at the Institute of Technology lunch counter and got work for two hours at noon. My afternoon's work, after the two hours of rush service, did not amount to much, and I began trying for something less strenuous.

There was at the school a certain Miss Ralston, much older than I, whose clothes, like mine, proclaimed the fact that her income was in inverse ratio to her aspirations, and to her I dared to speak of my wish to find work. She volunteered to seek advice from her sister who worked in one of Mrs. Quincy Shaw's day nurseries. As a result of her conference, she soon brought me word that there was a vacancy in one of the nurseries and that it would be wise for me to apply at once.

I felt that I was about to make a serious change in my program, and on my next trip to Brockton told my father that I had decided to leave the Museum School and attend classes in the evening. I explained that I had heard of a possible opening in one of Mrs. Shaw's nursery schools. The word *school* I added as it seemed to give a certain prestige to my statement. He was ill at the time with a severe attack of bronchitis, too ill indeed to argue against the project; and when I asked if he would get a note from Mr. William Lloyd Garrison, Jr., whom he knew, introducing me to the person who served as manager for certain of Mrs. Shaw's charities, he agreed to do so.

In due course the note arrived, addressed to the manager at her residence. Attired in my poor best, I presented myself at her door and was ushered into a sort of reception hall. I soon heard a swish of skirts and an elderly woman swept into the room, glared at me, and said, "What do you want?"

I faltered that I had heard she needed an attendant in one of the day nurseries.

"And you dared to come to my home to ask for work?" she shouted. "The place to apply for work is at one of the nurseries."

I started for the door. As I was going out I murmured that Mr. Garrison's letter had been addressed to her.

"Mr. Garrison," she said, in a changed tone, "why did you not tell me you had a letter from him? Give it to me."

I thrust it into her hand and ran from the house. I had never been spoken to in this manner before and I wept bitterly, walking through bystreets that I might not be seen.

Three days later I had a note from this person telling me to report at the nursery in the North Bennet Street Industrial School. There I was met by a large, rosy-faced woman who, having asked me more than twenty questions, told me I might begin work on Monday at half past eight. I was greatly elated. I could study three evenings a week, from seven until nine, at a school I had heard of where tuition was free. The three dollars a week, which the head person, after reading Mr. Garrison's letter, had specified as my salary, would help to pay my board, and undoubtedly I should soon be earning more. As a matter of fact, my check for the first four weeks was twenty-four dollars, double what I had expected. This I owed to the kind-hearted matron at the head of the nursery, who objected to paying only three dollars for the services I was asked to perform.

I can see again, as plainly as if I had gone to the nursery this morning, the great bare room with a sandbox in one corner and a row of little armchairs around the walls. In these chairs sat forty or more children, from year-and-a-half-old babies to four-year-old grown-ups. At the door sat the matron in blue dress and large white apron. She motioned me to be seated and began to sing,

The alder by the river
Shakes out her powdery curls
The willow buds in silver
For little boys and girls.[2]

Thin and clear like chirping sparrows the children sang with her, four or five songs in all they sang, and then the older ones went to kindergarten in the same building. The younger ones were marshaled around tables with checkerboard tops, where they were given beads to string, pegs and tiles with holes, blocks, and other means for pleasant and colorful occupation. The smallest babies were put to bed, or if very wakeful, allowed to sit in their little armchairs while several baby-loving young-sters amused them. It was my function to circulate among these lovable and easily pleased tots and perform the services that a nursemaid per-forms in any well-regulated family.

I shall never forget the one-year-old Celestina Mangioni who, from the time her hard-working mother brought her at eight in the morning, sat in her little chair, and when she was not sleeping, with her thin little legs sticking out in front of her opened her mouth in one long "yah-yah," which she seemed to continue without drawing a breath. She was the homeliest, most ill-conditioned, and most fretful baby I ever saw. Yet some years ago, when this same Celestina came to show us one of her own babies, she might well have posed for the Sistine Madonna, though not in the decidedly smart gown she wore. Her husband, a prosperous businessman, adores her, and they ride daily in their car, which was not made by Henry Ford.

The nursery babies' luncheon was a sight that people loved to see—long, low tables spread with clean linen cloths, on which were served nourishing soup with plenty of bread, an appetizing pudding, and as much milk as the babies could drink. After this repast the tots were marshaled into a long line, a singing line, and marched to the crib room.

I can still see that dusky, quiet, inner room, which none of the noises from the roaring streets could penetrate. There, in three long rows of small white cribs, the well-fed, sleepy babies were deposited. Some sang gently, others recited little scraps of baby poems, others fell asleep at once. Up and down, up and down the long aisles between the cribs I walked until all sounds had ceased and every baby was fast asleep; whereupon I sat down in a little chair beside the door until such time as the babies should wake.

After their sleep came the washing of little hands and faces, the combing of unruly hair, accompanied by loud but unavailing lamentations, followed by more games and singing, and then by the arrival of tired mothers who snatched their treasures to their breasts, murmured incoherent words of love and greeting, and bore them off, all the hard work and trials of the day forgotten as little hands smoothed lined cheeks and little voices cried joyously, "Going home." They were glad to be gone from the clean airy nursery to their dark, cheerless, tenement rooms, as long as mothers' arms were around them. I, who had lost my mother when about the age of these babies, hoped mightily that none of them might suffer my loss.

Once, or perhaps twice, during the years of my nursery service, I saw Mrs. Quincy Shaw, a woman with noble face and gentle bearing, who gave grandly and generously to many charities. I longed to speak to her, but how could a person who was earning six dollars a week address one who had millions. I did not try.

My father, feeling that he should be near me, gave up his work in Brockton, came to Boston, took a desk in the office of an old friend of Civil War times, and put the words "expert accountant" on his card. Little business came to him, and his Civil War pension of a few dollars a week provided him with a sum quite inadequate for his needs. We spent rather melancholy Sundays together in his tiny Columbus Avenue room.

I had made few acquaintances at the Art Museum, as I was conscious of my threadbare clothes and worn shoes, and of the fact that I had not that power which would cause my garments to be dubbed "marks of the eccentricity of genius."[3] I longed for companionship and, day after day, walked in my rest periods about the corridors of the museum, searching for someone of my own age who did not look prosperous. At last I found what I sought.

A pretty young thing, shy as a fawn, stood day after day with her eyes fixed on her work. Apparently no one spoke to her, and she apparently spoke to no one. I never saw her in other than the one red-and-black plaid dress, which like my own things, had evidently done good service for a long time. One day, in passing her easel, I spoke to her. She replied without raising her eyes. Every day after that first time, I spoke, and before long Edith Brown and I began taking walks together on Sunday afternoons.

Her sister, Agnes Brown, was a stenographer and, on fifteen dollars a week, she was paying living expenses for herself and her young sister and putting the latter through art school. I found that the two girls, who had recently come from their home in Nova Scotia, had taken an apartment on Batavia Street, in what was known as a "retired portion" of the Back Bay; and that there were two vacant rooms, which my father and I could have for a very modest sum. His room was known as a "side room," which had one front window; mine was a "well room," which meant that its only window opened upon the chimneylike well into which five other chambers and six bathrooms vented. I was given kitchen privileges, which made it possible to prepare our simple break-fasts. Of necessity I made my bed at once and opened a small folding table. There was just enough space for me to sit on the bed and for my father to occupy a chair against the wall on the other side of the table.

On Sunday morning, which was given over to cleaning rooms, doing mending, washing, and other odd jobs, my father, my two friends, and I would look forward to the afternoon, when we would go for a long walk through the parks or by the river. None of us could afford a car ride; that was a luxury to the deprivation of which I owe muscular legs, which today still carry me as far as I care to travel on them.

At the end of a long hot summer when no business had come to my father, we held a conference. His health, as well as his spirit, was broken. He had planned so many fine things when he had taken me from my grandfather's home, and what had come of them? From my point of view, many adventures; from his, many failures. So do the old and young differ in their points of view. As a result of our conference, he left Boston and went to board at a farm in Pepperell, Massachusetts, to regain his health, to observe nature, and to write poetry.

One afternoon as I stood at the head of the stairs watching the departure of mothers and babies, Miss Laliah B. Pingree, one of Mrs. Shaw's managers, happened to come in. As soon as I saw her, I felt that she had an understanding heart. She paused beside me and stood some minutes saying good-night to mothers and babies.

When all had gone she remarked, "You seem to me like a square peg in a round hole. Suppose you come to my apartment next Tuesday morning at ten, and we will talk over a little plan I have for you."

I could only nod my thanks. To be asked by a lady to go to her apartment was almost as great a shock, but of another kind, as it had been to be curtly dismissed at the beginning of my career. Half the night

I sat up sewing, patching, brushing and blacking my shoes and my somewhat rusty black straw hat to make myself presentable.

Miss Pingree put me at ease immediately and told me she would like me to take charge of certain girls' clubs she was forming, and of the girls' reading room maintained by the North Bennet Industrial School. As a result of this interview, I left the nursery, became leader of five girls' clubs, and had charge of the reading room two afternoons and two evenings each week. My salary was increased to eight dollars a week, and I felt richer the first week I took my pay envelope home than I had since the time I read copy at the Riverside Press. I was now a woman of independent means.

I was supposed to keep the girls off the street and to interest them in "something" so that their club night would always find them at the neighborhood house. I had intelligence enough to know that I was entirely inadequate for the task, but as I had to earn my bread, I argued somewhat as follows, "I know life has far more to offer than I have yet found. Undoubtedly these girls feel the same way about it. Perhaps we can find together the key to some secret garden in which we can profitably enjoy ourselves."

The club at one "neighborhood house" was composed of riotous colored girls, the average age of the members being about fourteen years. They were excellent mimics, and I learned much by watching their imitations of me when they thought I was not looking.

The North Bennet Street club was a mixture of Irish, Italian, and Jewish girls, the Jewish element predominating. Strangely enough the girls got along together perfectly, better by far than those clubs composed solely of Irish Americans at three other neighborhood houses.

When I met my first club, I asked the girls, after the manner of all inexperienced club leaders, what they would like to do, and with one voice they replied, "Elect officers." The matter of choosing a president, vice-president, and secretary occupied about an hour. The business of collecting pennies with which to buy blank books for the secretary and treasurer and the making of plans for a party occupied the next hour. At nine o'clock I was bidden "good-bye, teacher," in a ringing chorus by the club members as they adjourned. This first meeting was typical of all other first meetings, and from that time on, parties and picnics were continually being planned and discussed.

In those days, remember, there were no radios, few motion picture theaters, and very few automobiles. There was neither subway nor elevated, and the horse cars with loose straw to keep one's feet warm still ran on Newbury Street. A Christmas party, therefore, with a tree and a play acted by club members, followed by dancing, games, and ice cream in paper saucers, was an event looked forward to from September till Christmas. These parties could not come off until after the twenty-sixth, as we had to depend on trees the churches had used the day before. From January until June, funds were accumulated for a picnic at Waverly Oaks or Revere Beach. Once, we got together a sufficient amount to go to Salem Willows—a day forever impressed on my memory, for the sea was rough and twenty-seven of my charges were stretched out wherever room could be found, greenly seasick.

What did we do besides plan for parties? I try to lift the veil that obscures the memory of what else transpired at the meetings, but all I can recall is ploddingly getting ready from after breakfast until half past three for the afternoon clubs, which met from four till six, and for the evening clubs, which met from seven till nine. I always arrived at the neighborhood house cold with terror lest the girls had decided not to come. One meeting over, I rushed to the next place, where I was given a meal that I could not enjoy because of the ever-present fear that seven o'clock would find me alone, the girls off to find diversion in some other quarter.

Sometimes on winter evenings, when I pass the cold corners where I waited for streetcars after my evening was over, I thank God that I had the real adventure of being ill-clad, ill-fed, ill-sheltered, and friendless but for Edith and Agnes, two dear girls as poor as myself, who had taken me in. I am grateful for this experience, which makes it easier for me to get the point of view of the girl who is literally on her own.

In due course my friend Edith Brown graduated from the Art Museum, and I proposed to the various nursery heads that she give drawing lessons at the clubs. This was approved, and she started earning a very modest weekly amount.

What was my surprise on going home one day to find my beloved aunt and uncle in the living room of our little apartment. About fifteen years had passed since I had seen or heard from them. Our joy at meeting was mutual. They told me with heavy hearts that they had followed my adventures, but that out of respect for my father's wishes, they had never tried to see me. They were still living in Concord and wanted me to come to see them the following Sunday. This I was delighted to do, and from that day until I parted company with them in this life, I saw them frequently and knew that I had their dear love as they had mine; and my father once more visited at their home.

Shortly after this meeting with my aunt and uncle, Agnes Brown decided to give up her apartment and leave Boston. Edith Brown and I, therefore, took a back room at three dollars and fifty cents a week in a rooming house on Massachusetts Avenue. It had, as I recall, a folding bed that featured as a wardrobe by day and as a bed by night. The room was furnished, also, with a marble-topped table, several chairs, and a bureau. We had the use of a closet, which contained a marble washbasin with hot and cold water faucets. All our meals, except those that we had at the neighborhood houses, we got in this room. We had a small, one-burner gas stove, which could be attached to the light tip by a rubber tube, a device long since declared unsafe. In this room we lived for more than a year. Then, my aunt and uncle having made me an allowance of twenty-five dollars a month, we moved into a front room on the top floor of a rooming house on St. James Avenue, which stood where the building of the John Hancock Life Insurance Company now stands. This was an expensive room, which cost us five dollars a week. It had a bay window from which we could look down into the garden of the Notre Dame Academy, where lilacs bloomed in the spring and birds sang, and where in winter the snow remained pure and white on trees, bushes, and grass plot.

As the population of the North End gradually changed from Irish to Jewish, the reading room over which I presided two afternoons and two evenings weekly became so popular that it was decided to open it every afternoon and every evening. I therefore gave up my clubs in order to spend all my time in the reading room.

Out of my eight-dollar salary and my twenty-five-dollar monthly allowance, I was able to help my father, as well as to lay aside a small sum every week in the Suffolk Bank for Seamen and Others. Edith Brown still taught drawing lessons at the clubs and in addition had several regular classes at the North Bennet Industrial School. We were in such affluent circumstances that we were able occasionally to take an all-day trip.

On a Sunday morning we would have an early breakfast. This we achieved by placing a woven wire mat on top of the gas globe. On this mat we set the coffee pot, into which we dropped two well-washed eggs. After the coffee and eggs were cooked, we toasted bread on the wire mat; and where, I ask, could one find a more satisfying meal than buttered toast, steaming coffee, and eggs cooked to a turn?

By eight o'clock, breakfast eaten, dishes washed, and bed made, we were on our way to Nahant, or to Belmont, or to Arlington Heights. Nahant meant an all-day trip. We had a trolley ride across the marshes to Lynn, then a walk along the narrow strip of sandy beach that connected Little Nahant with the mainland, and from Little Nahant another beach walk to Big Nahant, right out in the ocean. We knew a cliff trail that led down to the sea, past pools where delicate sea anemones clung to the rocks, and where no human habitations were visible. In some sheltered spot we would sit for hours reading aloud and talking of distant lands across the Atlantic that we hoped some day to visit. In Belmont there were cedar-clad uplands, so thickly strewn with outcroppings of pudding-stone ledges that one could seem as far from a city as in New Hampshire hills. At Arlington Heights we had discovered a patch of marshy woods where from spring to fall the wildflowers of the season seemed to wait our coming. Lack of funds never meant to us lack of holidays packed with happy adventures.

Occasionally we treated ourselves to a weekend trip; then what a glorious holiday we had! On one such occasion we took a boat on Saturday afternoon to Gloucester for seventy-five cents apiece. There we succeeded in getting a room for two nights at one dollar a night. Fortunately Sunday turned out to be a very fine day, so we rose at five o'clock to take a trolley to Annisquam, where, at a fisherman's eating house, we had thick coffee in thick mugs, and very thick cream-of-tartar biscuits with thin butter. The rest of the day we walked, reveling in the colors of sea, and earth, and sky. We followed the shore from Annisquam back again to Gloucester, some twenty-five miles, and at about eight o'clock in the evening limped into a restaurant where we ate quantities of applesauce and bread and butter, and then limped on to our one-dollar-room, well content.

I have forgotten to mention that during my very poorest days at the YWCA I had received from the *Boston Evening Transcript* a check for fifteen dollars in payment for a description of a Portuguese festival that I had witnessed in the old Portuguese church on North Bennet Street. This unexpected windfall encouraged me to think that perhaps I could learn to write. Thenceforward, for some years I earned a few dollars now and again by writing descriptive articles.

One summer I thought we might earn a vacation by that means, and a newspaper actually did give us water and rail transportation from Boston to the Evangeline country and back, in payment for a series of travel articles to be written by me and illustrated by Edith Brown. We had our board and lodging to pay for and scanty were the funds we felt justified in allowing for the purpose—twenty-five dollars apiece I think the amount totaled. This allowed one dollar and fifty cents a day for lodgings, fifteen cents each for two meals and twenty-five cents for one, and left each of us about six dollars for emergencies. It took some financing to get along on that amount, but we did it, and landed back in Boston with a capital of thirty-five cents between us. We had seen Yarmouth, Halifax, Grand Pre, Digby, the Annapolis Valley, and Cape Blomidon.

The appearance of the travel articles in the *New Bedford Standard* encouraged me to enter a class in English at Radcliffe College. Professor Charles T. Copeland conducted this class in his own inimitable manner. His trifling mannerisms did not obscure the big vision he presented of the beauty and grandeur of English literature.

In 1899 our reading room became a deposit station of the Boston Public Library. My title was changed to Custodian of Station W of the Boston Public Library, my salary was increased to forty dollars a month, and I was required, to my great delight, to attend the regular monthly meetings with other custodians at the Central Library.

Although the reading room was a regularly recognized station of the Boston Public Library, the school authorities continued to interest themselves in the social service aspect of the work, which was under the direct supervision of a committee chosen by the Board of Managers. The chairman of this committee, Mrs. James Jackson Storrow, a Boston philanthropist, was brimful of goodwill, good deeds, and common sense. The latter quality led her to investigate the library; and one July afternoon, when the thermometer registered in the nineties, I entered the reading room to find her clad in a white linen suit, waiting for me. She asked me about different procedures and begged to be given some work, which she went at with eager interest. Of all her many kind actions, that one stands out in my memory. Earnestly as we may believe in democracy, there is in most of us a sneaking something that causes us to feel it a more democratic act for the person of vast wealth to show us good fellowship than for the scrubwoman to make a like gesture.

Before she left, Mrs. Storrow told me that she was going to England for six weeks. She said she did not want to close her country house and let the servants go, and she asked if some of my friends and I would accommodate her by staying there during her absence. Next day I went to see her long rambling house on a high hill overlooking the Charles River valley. The gardens and groves of the estate, carefully laid out by a landscape architect, had made it a kind of fairyland one dreams of, but seldom sees.

Edith and I at once gave up our St. James Avenue room; I sent for my father and two friends to join us, and we entered upon a life of ease that well-nigh made us forget that hardships were jolly adventures. The food bills were all that disturbed our peace. I recall now two items for the first week, namely, ninety quarts of milk and fourteen dozen eggs. The servants did the ordering and we "lived high." However, we had no room rent, and when the food bills were divided among five people, it was not so bad.

My father reveled in the beauty of the place and produced poems to his heart's content. As for me, since my tenth year I had not known the sense of well-being that stole over me as I sat after dinner on the broad veranda with "my family," watching the moon rise above the distant hills and hearing the owls hooting in the nearby woods. That experience left me with a quenchless ambition to acquire a home; and when we broke up I told my father, as I saw him aboard the train on his return trip to Pepperell, that I would try to provide him with one before another twelve months had passed. Just how this was to be done I did not know, but I had faith that the thing was right and therefore must come to pass.

Here let me read an advertisement in the *Transcript*. "Wanted a responsible person to occupy a furnished house from June 1 till October 1, and to answer a doctor's telephone." It was a home for a few months only, but what an opportunity. I answered the advertisement, with the result that my father, Edith, and I were soon installed in one-half of a big, comfortable double house in Brookline. My father, being at home all day, was put in charge of the doctor's telephone.

My first act was to plant ten cents worth of nasturtium seeds in the little garden plot under the doctor's windows. They throve and blossomed riotously. It was the first garden of my own since Kendall days; and it seemed to me the flowers were larger and the colors more choice than those of any nasturtiums I had ever seen.

How good the breakfasts tasted and the dinners, which we had at noon as I was due in the library at two. My father managed his own supper, as both Edith and I were away. It was a happy summer, and when the first of October came and Father went back to Pepperell and Edith and I to St. James Avenue, I encouraged him by saying that the next time he came, it would be to a home for winter as well as summer.

Christmas and other public holidays I spent with him at the farm at which he boarded in Pepperell. By this time I had become quite a financier, and as I had regularly deposited small sums in the bank, I had a little ahead. I reported this to my father and he at once began looking for a cottage in Pepperell. He still had his dream that if he had a little home in the country, he could live quite satisfactorily on his pension. I did not wish to discourage him, and when he reported that he had found a tiny three-room house for sale, I bought it. This transaction gave my father a new lease on life. The plans he made for remodeling it occupied most of his time. I think he must have become acquainted with every tree, bush, and vine on the small plot of ground that surrounded the house. He also loved the woods that bordered our land on one side. There in the silence, unbroken save by the call of a bird or the song of the wind in the treetops, he would lie for hours on a carpet of pine needles, inches deep, and plan our lives as they would be lived in the little three-room house. With his pension money and the twenty-five dollars a month I had from Aunt Anna, we could get on very nicely, he said.

In March the Misses Martin wrote that they were giving up their half of the house in which we had lived the previous summer, that the doctor was satisfied with the service we had given, and that he would be glad to have us take the house permanently. I closed the offer immediately and then set about solving the problem of financing the undertaking.

The debit side of the sheet, according to my estimate, came out by the week approximately as follows:

Rent	$ 5.75
Food	
(Father, E., myself, maid)	14.00
Maid (wages)	5.00
Light and gas stove	1.00
Coal range and furnace	1.50
Incidentals	2.00
	$29.25

My father could not pay over six dollars a week, so this left twenty-three dollars and twenty-five cents for Edith and me. Impossible! It was clear that I must have some boarders.

We had six bedrooms; I could spare three. Therefore, three boarders must be found. I made another calculation. With three extra people, ten dollars and fifty cents for food and fifty cents for light must be added to the expense sheet, making a total of forty dollars and twenty-five cents. The three boarders, Edith, and I would pay seven dollars, and my father six dollars, making forty-one dollars, which allowed a margin of seventy-five cents a week as a sinking fund. Nothing was lacking for the successful working of the scheme but three boarders and the necessary furnishings. My first step was to present the case to Miss Lavinia Gould, superintendent of the North Bennet Street Industrial School, where I served as librarian.

"Have you any idea of how one acquires boarders?" I asked.

She said she thought that it would be well to advertise. Then she questioned me about the house and ended by saying, "I'll be one of your boarders, and I'll bring all the furniture for my room."

Encouraged by this success, I next approached one of the teachers at the school who said that she lived at home, but she suggested the names of two other teachers who might like to join my cooperative scheme. They were not only willing to come, but they likewise agreed to bring their own furniture. Thus our household was made complete. Never have I seen anything like the bareness of that house when the Misses Martin's furniture had been moved. The kitchen was less bare than any other room, as it had a gas stove and a range with two rows of cheerful red bricks in front of it like a rug. The dining room and the cupboard were bare to the point of bleakness. Mother Hubbard's dog would have fled from them, howling. Fortunately the doctor's office, at the right side of the door, was beautifully furnished and carpeted with a fine blue carpet.

Of the six bedrooms, we had to furnish four. Then there was the sitting room on the second floor, which must have at least a few chairs. We were puzzled, but not dismayed. The rooms had to be furnished; therefore, they would be furnished and they were. We may have had a few packing boxes with chintz curtains in front of them for tables; we may have picked up the bureaus for a dollar apiece at the secondhand shops; we may have had only cots instead of bedsteads; and our mattresses may have been stuffed with excelsior in lieu of hair, but what did it matter? As for the other rooms, Aunt Anna found in her attic all we needed, even dishes and pots and pans. For floors, we became experts in the painting line, and rugs would only have meant extra shaking and sweeping. Toward the end of the month I secured a maid from an employment office, and by October first our home was ready.

To be sure, it was a harder life than I had led when I had no home responsibilities. In addition to my work at the library, I now had the planning of meals, the marketing, the keeping of accounts, and the paying of bills. My planning had to be done and the marketing accomplished before I left home for the library at one o'clock.

In the early spring of 1903, I received a letter containing a check for three hundred odd dollars, my share from the French settlement for destruction of one of my great-great-grandfather's ships during the War of 1812. I had never heard of the French claims, and on reading the slip that accompanied the check, I experienced as great a thrill as if I had fallen heir to a million dollars. My father was comfortably provided for; we had a good maid, and dear Miss Gould would gladly, I knew, serve as head of the house. As for the other two boarders, they had gone to their farm for the summer. I asked for three months' leave from the library and got it, with the assumption that travel in Italy would make me a more valuable worker. Edith and I started for Italy.

We sailed on a very old liner, which carried only twelve cabin passengers, and over seven hundred men, women, and children in the steerage. The captain and the other officers were most agreeable, which is more than I can say for the odors that arose from the seven hundred steerage passengers below our deck. Whichever way the wind blew we got a stench that "all the perfumes of Araby" could not have sweetened. We were glad to land at Naples.

From a study of our *Rest Tour Book* we had decided upon the convent of Les Soeurs d'Espérance as our stopping place. As soon as we were through customs, we entered a quaint little gig drawn by a horse who wore on his head a plume, behind his ears several artificial flowers, and at his throat a jingling bell. Through many narrow alleys, in what appeared to be a poor part of the city, we turned and twisted between high walls. Finally we drew up before a gate with a hole in the middle, through which the driver reached his hand and pulled an invisible rope that set distant bells ringing and brought a sweet-faced nun to the gate. As it closed behind us, and we walked under blossoming oleanders toward the open doorway of the convent, we seemed to have turned the page of an old Book of Hours, from which a picture had come to life.

To tell of our travels would be like reciting pages from a guidebook. Suffice it to say that we enjoyed to the full strolling on Santa Lucia, "doing" the museums and galleries with conscientious thoroughness, driving to Pozzuoli and Baia, and walking on the shores of Lake Avernus. The day in Pompeii was better even than Lytton's romance,[4] a childhood favorite. As for the drive from Castellammare along the Gulf of Salerno to Amalfi, those who have taken it will agree that words have never yet done it justice.

After a charming ten days in Sorrento at the Cocumella Hotel, formerly a monastery, we went to Rome where we started out to tour galleries and churches. We had scarcely emerged from a trip through the catacombs when the tolling of the great bell in the Campanile announced that the only messenger who then had power to call a pope from his voluntary prison had spoken, and that the old prelate had at last gone beyond the walls of the Vatican gardens.

Next day the plaza of Saint Peter's was packed with people of many nationalities who had assembled in Rome when it was known that Leo XIII was nearing his end. We joined the vast crowd that gradually lengthened itself into a narrow, multicolored ribbon that moved slowly but surely toward the cathedral's entrance, to be swallowed up bit by bit in the gloom beyond the portico. We moved past the chapel in which the tired old man lay with a smile upon his face, as if asleep. Around him stood the Swiss Guards in their picturesque uniforms, guarding his mortal body for the last time.

The passing of the pope meant the closing of galleries and churches. Because of this we left Rome after a morning in the Forum, a lovely afternoon on the Janiculum hill, and a half hour in the English cemetery, where we looked reverently at the graves of Keats and Shelley. We then journeyed on to Florence, and thence to Assisi, where we followed Saint Francis from the little Portiuncula in the vast Cathedral of Saint Mary of the Angels, up through Assisi to the monastery, known as the Carcere, perched on the brow of a chestnut-clad height. After a few days we journeyed to Bologna and thence to Ferrara, the birthplace of Savonarola and the last home of the poet Tasso. But the climax of this journey came when we crossed the Adriatic Causeway about midnight and entered Venice on such a night as young Jessica and Lorenzo describe.[5] By way of Milan and Genoa we returned to Naples, where we boarded the liner for America.

We had been overjoyed at going, and we were equally overjoyed at returning. My father had decorated all the rooms with nasturtiums, and Miss Gould had arranged to have hot cornbread for tea because she knew the Europeans did not know how to make this New England delicacy, and indeed she was right, as far as we could tell. Not since we had left our homeland had we tasted anything half so good.

As soon as we were settled again, I began to spend weekends with my aunt and uncle in Concord; and the summer after our trip abroad, Edith and I were invited to spend a fortnight with them at their cottage in Nonquitt near New Bedford. While there, they told me that it had been decided to allow me the income that would have been my mother's had she lived. This meant a variable amount, from fifty to seventy-five dollars a month, as the income from investments varied. Thus was the fear of a poverty-stricken old age removed from my dear father, and he began writing poetry with renewed zeal, and planning trips north, south, east, and west. As for me, following Benjamin Franklin's maxims, I began to accumulate a fund for the purchase of a home of our own in or near Boston, as I had no desire to live in our Pepperell cottage, which I usually rented for the summer.

In spite of the wealth that had come to me, I had no intention of giving up library work. At first I had hesitated before choosing this profession, for the reason that I did not wish to be responsible for giving to young people some of the trash I had myself obtained from public libraries. This qualm had been silenced by logical reasoning. I felt that there was not as much trash in a public library as there was on a newsstand. Furthermore, there was always the opportunity of quietly offering the best, whether it was accepted or not. Again, who was I to set myself up as an infallible judge of good or bad literature. Perhaps my tastes were not sufficiently catholic. After all, I had read much trash and forgotten it; other young people would be pretty sure to do the same thing.

I had as free time every Sunday, all public holidays, and a month in summer. Some of this time I devoted to the search for a lot on which to build a house. I had a feeling that it was right to have a house of our own in or near Boston and that the money would be forthcoming when I needed it. I was not mistaken. Shortly after I had found a satisfactory lot, a piece of property belonging to my grandfather's estate was sold, and one-fourth of the amount was sent to me. With this money I was able to buy the lot, which was situated in Chestnut Hill, a part of Brookline, Massachusetts. It was almost the only vacant lot thereabouts. The neighborhood was well developed; the houses were all single, surrounded by attractive gardens, and immediately behind my lot were the Chestnut Hill golf links, acres of beautifully kept grounds, edged by clumps of tall pines.

Uncle Walton, who had many artist friends, gave me a letter of introduction to a well-known firm of architects, who designed a small attractive house and supervised its building with as much care, and with as great interest, as if I had commissioned them to build a palace. Of course, I had to go deeply into debt, but the person who lent me the money was amply protected, and it was good for me to have to save money, as our three-hundred-dollar trip abroad had made me rather reckless.

The house, which was started in May, was finished in September, and when we moved to our own home, I had the feeling that I had traveled fast and far in the years since I had left the "well room" at Batavia Street.

Ever since becoming a librarian, I had been disturbed by the reading habits—or lack of reading habits—of the library's patrons, especially of the young girls. They took a book one day and returned it the next. In short, they never read a book through, and called only for fairy tales. Andrew Lang's blue, pink, red, yellow, and other colored fairy books, they read to tatters. After thinking long about this matter, I started a story hour. The library closed at six o'clock on Saturday evenings, and seven o'clock was the hour I chose to begin storytelling. Before many months had gone by, I noticed that the same girls were coming every Saturday night. Soon they declared for an organization, went through the customary procedure of electing a president, vice-president, secretary, and treasurer, gave themselves the name of "Saturday Evening Girls," and developed what everyone spoke of as a wonderful club spirit. I had no objection to the organization, but I thought the machinery should turn out something besides the story hour and a few parties, so I made the girls a speech somewhat as follows: "Some day you girls are going to enter the business world. You will need to know how to use the tool called mind, so that you can do your own thinking. You will need to know how to cooperate, and how to give and take with good-humored self-control. You will need to have a well-informed mind, and if you are to win positions with people you can respect and admire, you will need to have a sense of the values of good literature, good music, and good recreation." I then proposed the following program to occupy the time from seven to nine on Saturdays: "From 7:00 to 7:30 we shall have a business meeting; from 7:30 to 8:00 someone will tell a story; from 8:00 to 8:30 we shall sing; from 8:30 to 9:00 we shall dance or play games." This program "took"; indeed, it took so well that I was given an assistant in the library and allowed time on several afternoons after school hours for other clubs.

When the clubs had been running several years, Mrs. Storrow offered us the use of an old farmhouse at Plymouth for the summer. The result of this experiment was so satisfactory that she bought an acre at Wingaersheek Beach, West Gloucester. Through the middle of this piece of ground, which was covered with a tangle of barberry, wild smilax, and bittersweet, ran a flat granite ledge from which there was a view of the marshes, the dunes, and the sea. Beside this great rock, as if by magic, rose a camp house with fourteen bedrooms, a large living room, and a tiny kitchen. Roofed and screened verandas on all four side of the house, upstairs and down, made outdoor living possible.

The carpenters completed the building about the middle of June, and Miss Sally Beck, the North End "school visitor" who had been interested in the clubs for years, Miss Winship, an assistant in the library, and I went down to get ready for the first fourteen girls. We took with us provisions and utensils that we had been accumulating. We took also Miss Beck's cat, Trifles, and mongrel dog, Jimmy Jocks.

The "deepo" wagon had no sooner left us at the camp than one discovery began to tread on the heels of another. The cookstove had not arrived. The fireplace chimney refused to draw and filled the rooms with blinding smoke. Our one-burner Florence oil stove was of no avail as we had forgotten to bring kerosene. The well was not finished, and the nearest fresh water was a mile away. The workmen had left without putting in the wire screens, and marsh mosquitoes devoured us by day and by night. The two weeks spent in attacking and overcoming difficulties were packed with unexpected adventures.

Then, all of a sudden, everything straightened out. The cookstove arrived; the fireplace began to draw; the well was finished; the screens were up; the furniture and dishes were in place; seventeen beds were made, with an extra blanket rolled at the foot of each; and Bella Napoli, the cow, Jerusalem, the horse, and The Golden, a democrat wagon, were in the barn.

It was five o'clock of a perfect July afternoon when the deepo wagon deposited the first fourteen girls at the door. A huge pot of spaghetti and a saucepan of prunes simmered on the stove, a batch of oatmeal bread was baking in the oven, the table in the living room was laid, and on the mantelpiece above the fireplace was a blue bowl filled with wild roses. As the girls came in, staggering under bulging suitcases, the three of us, after the manner of one of America's earliest inhabitants, cried, "Welcome!"

Then said the practical Miss Beck, "Now girls, select your rooms, wash your hands and faces, and come to supper."

The girls piled upstairs and clumped up and down the wooden corridors choosing their rooms so that comrades would not be separated. This done, they clattered downstairs, sat down at the table, and did justice to the simple fare provided.

Those who summered at the camp year after year say that they never knew a dull moment. Miss Beck taught them how to row, how to swim, and how to cook. There was no hired help. Each girl, on arrival, found her name on the work schedule, which was changed every few days so that no one girl had all the prize jobs. The girls worked with enthusiasm, and no matter how unexpectedly anyone arrived, the house would be found in order, with good food in preparation and fresh flowers on the mantelpiece. There were sailing trips, hikes, and picnics in the dunes, where coffee was cooked over a driftwood fire; there were clamming trips on the mud flats behind the dunes and huckleberry-picking races on the hill. Best of all, friendships were formed that endured and grew stronger with the years. The success of the camp was due to Miss Beck, large-hearted, generous, untiring, and overflowing with the pure enjoyment of living. She had no interest in the uplift business, she saw no problem in the girls, and she had no purpose other than that of giving her charges a good time, and of having a good time with them.

At my home, things had not been going smoothly. My father had become quite irresponsible. He was often gone from home for hours at a time, we knew not where. I was finally told I must place him where he would have expert care. His condition was the result of hardships endured in the Civil War. For weeks he had served under the broiling southern sun in the trenches, before Fort Sumpter. He had acted as assistant adjutant general of a post in the Florida swamps. He had been wounded at Gaines Mill and captured. For six weeks he had lain in Libby Prison, an experience he refused to talk about. I took him, myself, to a well-managed private hospital near Boston, where I could call on him at any time. There he had a pleasant room, the best of care, and a garden in which to walk.[6]

He was one of the gentlest of men, never so happy as when listening to the songs of birds, or cultivating a garden plot, or composing sonnets as he walked in the woods or by the river. His two terrible years at the front, performing services so foreign to his nature, had left a wound that bit deeper and deeper into his mind as the years went by, until his death a few years later.

When he entered the hospital, the house became a lonesome place.

George Guerrier in old age. Reproduced courtesy of the Whaling Museum, New Bedford, Massachusetts.

His comfort had been my object for so many years that with his departure I was like a parent who had lost her child. Mrs. Storrow, who knew
something of my troubles, decided to send Edith and me off for a
vacation, and before we knew what was happening, we were aboard a
liner sailing for Rotterdam.

In my childhood I had owned a Noah's Ark filled with neatly painted
animals, trees, bushes, and a few houses. When I first looked upon
the banks of the Scheldt, I thought I was having a sort of Alice-in-
Wonderland experience and had become one of the figures in a life-size
Noah's Ark. The meadows were picture-book green, the trees were
neatly trimmed, the red-and-white houses as clean as those of Spotless
Town, the hens and cows tidy beyond belief, and the people were really
and truly in "costume" going about their daily business.

Dordrecht was our first stop after leaving the boat. We arrived late in
the evening at the inn, and with a sigh of satisfaction fell asleep in plump
feather beds. Early in the morning we were awakened by sounds that
reminded me of the tin peddler's cart of my childhood. It proceeded
from a sure-enough dogcart. The dog, a perfect Patrasche for patience
and intelligence, was harnessed to a cart filled with shining brass milk
cans.

Dordrecht offered many attractions, but we were out for the extreme
in atmosphere, and at Rijsoord we had been told we should find it.
Rijsoord was a tiny collection of small houses set down in a wide flat
plain, crosshatched by innumerable canals. The one hostelry recom-
mended by our Rest Tour Book had no room vacant. However, the
cheerful landlady allowed us to deposit our bags and sent one of her
daughters, who spoke English as well as Dutch, with us to see if we
could get rooms at the "clomper's shop," that is, the shop of a maker of
wooden shoes.

Above this shop was a species of loft with a long aisle through the
middle, with small cubicles on either side furnished with "American"
beds and washstands. The iron bedsteads, in lieu of springs, had wide
iron slats running from side to side. In order to prevent them from
sagging, they were fully three inches higher in the middle than at the
sides. The mattress was stuffed with cornhusks and cobs, and the trick
was to balance oneself on the peak, as all real Americans were supposed
to do. We found it easier to put the mattress on the floor and submit our
bodies as dance and banquet halls for fleas, thick as the sand on West
Gloucester shores. Nevertheless, we slept.

On pouring water into my tin basin in the morning, I found it filled with wiggling polliwogs, which made it necessary to strain the water through a pocket handkerchief. After the first morning we told our landlady that Americans had a habit of washing in boiled water. She shook her head and clucked her tongue; nevertheless, next morning we had our polliwogs boiled, with the result that they were strained more easily. The girl who spoke English explained to us the usefulness of a canal system. From the little scum-covered line of water that fenced the clomper's shop, water was drawn for drinking, washing, and laundering, and there was no need for any dirt to accumulate anywhere, as it was thrown into the canal and carried away. This information was given, it must be remembered, more than fifty years ago. I have no doubt that by this time the uses of canal water have been somewhat curtailed. In any case, I have never seen people who looked healthier and happier than the canal users of Rijsoord.

Our travel cinema rapidly unrolled and showed us The Hague; Haarlem with its tulip fields, its Frans Hals galleries, and its memories of Coster; Leyden with its bare church and its historic association with the Prince of Orange and the Pilgrim Fathers; Amsterdam; and the trips to Marken, a perpetual opera bouffe, Volendam and Edam with their display of round rosy cheeses and of cattle in barns, with lace curtains at the windows.

It was a restful change to sit still in the train between Amsterdam and Utrecht, and to feast our eyes on the fields of purple heather, which carpeted the ground as far as the eye could see. From Utrecht we traveled to Cologne and had a room directly opposite the cathedral. There was bright moonlight, and till long past midnight we sat on the deep window ledge, silently absorbing the beauty of the storied stones.

Our two days on the Rhine, between vineyards and castellated heights, were unmarred by rain or fog. The inn at Ehrenbreitstein faced the grim old fortress, and we could see the bridge of boats swinging gently with the tide.

Strasbourg did not please us, probably because of a downpour of rain that swept round the street corners in gusts and kept us damp and cold. The people seemed discontented and far from cordial. Sight-seeing became a dreary business, to be gone through to the bitter end. The verger, instead of allowing us to leave the cathedral and go in search of a cup of hot coffee, herded us with a crowd of other persons into an anteroom at half past eleven and shut the door while he collected fees for allowing us to stand in the presence of the old clock, around the face of which at noon marched twelve peglike wooden "apostles."

Heidelberg's enchanting castle, where we spent a day and where we ate a paper-bag luncheon of black bread and cheese, and great bunches of deep purple grapes, erased the memory of our dour day in Strasbourg with the magic beauty of its lovely setting. The stone walls of the castle were completely clothed with ivy; even the terraces were hidden by a carpet of dark green leaves. A peaceful and a lovely sight it was, with the protecting heights above it and the slow-moving river at its feet.

We entered Switzerland by way of Basle and hurried on to Lucerne, pausing for a day's sail on the lake among scenes sacred to the name of Wilhelm Tell. From Lucerne we rode over the Brünig pass to Interlaken, and from Interlaken to Wilderswil. It was dusk when we arrived at the chalet, and on entering our rooms, Edith went at once to the casement window and opened it wide. There in the distance was the peak of the Jungfrau, crowned with everlasting snow. Below this peak, dark firs clothed the sides of the valley of Wilderswil. The silence was unbroken save by the thunder of the glacial torrent that pierced the wall of the forest and came tumbling to the floor of the vale.

We walked to Grindelwald and picked edelweiss on the edge of its great glacier. We climbed to lovely Mürren; on its plateau we spent a long afternoon lying on an upland slope covered with pink crocuses. We sailed the Thuner See and visited a little pottery in the midst of a field of crimson-tipped daisies. We rested in an arbor overlooking the lake and the distant Alps, and as we sat, a company of choirboys filed into a nearby church and with well-trained voices sang Gounod's "Ave Maria." The end of a perfect day came as we sailed back along the Thuner See and saw the rosy alpine glow touch the peaks with a heavenly radiance.

The next day as we walked through the Lauterbrunnen Valley, we talked of the West Gloucester camp, and of the possibility of starting an industry at which girls, not able to afford the camp fees, could work and earn the small sum that the two weeks' vacation cost. We spoke of making marmalade, or fruitcake, of hemming napkins and dish towels, and finally, we spoke of pottery, of the charming peasant ware of Italy, of Holland, of Germany, and now of Switzerland. Since our club girls were almost all of peasant stock, why not start an art pottery and produce an American peasant ware?

The pottery that came into being as a result of this visionary idea was, therefore, the direct descendant of the Swiss pottery in the field of crimson-tipped daisies beside the Thuner See.

Edith and I had talked about our pottery scheme on the return voyage, and when we got home we made it our business to find out where we could learn throwing, glazing, and firing. In the Charlestown pottery, a rambling, rickety shack where demijohns were made, we found a Swedish potter who, when under the influence of liquor, "threw" like an inspired demon. From him we learned to "throw." We then bought a kick wheel from the old Merrimac Pottery at Newburyport. Gus Melton, a maker of bean pots in a Cambridge pottery, set up our wheel in the cellar of the Chestnut Hill house and gave us further lessons in the art of throwing. When the cellar was well stocked with little gray bowls drying on shelves, on window sills, and on the floor, we sought out a pottery chemist who, for a substantial consideration, parted with some of his formulas, which we found later on in a printed book of formulas in our own public library.

After studying the catalogs devoted to kilns and consulting the architect of our house as to whether or not the chimney would carry off the smoke, we ordered a small oil-burning kiln and had it set up in the cellar. It weighed a ton, it was very awkward to handle, and three men worked an entire day to get it off the express wagon, through the door yard, and into the cellar. The first bright blue glazed tiles that came out of the kiln I carried around with me for weeks, showing them to all my acquaintances as the most remarkable of ceramic productions.

During that fall and winter we spent most of our spare time at home in the cellar. Although it was very cold, as the clay was wet, and the floor was slimy with it, neither cold nor wetness could suppress the creative thrills we experienced, as shapeless masses of clay centered and whirled into shape under our hands. The words we stuck up in our little workshop were chosen from *The Nürnberg Stove:* "We derive all the value in us from the fact that our makers wrought at us with zeal, with integrity, with faith to do nobly an honest thing."[7]

During the summer vacation many girls from the library clubs came to practice pottery making with us at Chestnut Hill. To what end? Always the end was a little pottery in a garden where flowers would bloom from April to November, and where from November to April in warm, well-lighted rooms, the girls would work happily at their benches. It was a fair dream, and that it would come true, we never doubted. Mrs. Storrow, who had continued to manifest interest in the clubs, came frequently to visit the potters in the Chestnut Hill cellar. She was almost as excited as we were when the first glazed pieces were drawn from the kiln. With enthusiastic generosity she bought a house on Hull Street opposite Copp's Hill Burying Ground in the old North End and had it remodeled for the use of the clubs and the pottery.

In the front basement, entered from the street, there was a shop where the pottery was to be sold. The rest of the basement was given over to shower baths, a furnace room, and a kiln room. On the first floor was a club room and the pottery workroom. The second floor, one large room with open fireplace, was planned for an assembly room. The two upper floors were charming little apartments, three bedrooms, a living room, kitchen, and bath. Above all was a roof garden.

When the house was furnished and ready for occupancy, the question arose as to who should live in it and direct its activities. No one could be found, so it worked out that Edith and I rented our Chestnut Hill house to friends, our housemates found other quarters, and we took one of the model apartments at a rental of twenty-five dollars a month. I was to serve as director and Edith was to develop the pottery, which was to be called the Paul Revere Pottery, because it was located within a stone's throw of the Old North Church, famous since the night of 18 April 1775.

After I had agreed to act as director of the clubhouse, I sat down to consider what qualifications I had for the job and to review my experiences. I remembered that my first attempt at "doing good" had occurred in my YWCA days, when I was yet so poor that I had not the price of a five-cent carfare to spare. I had offered my services as teacher in a Sunday school in the North End Union on Parmenter Street,[8] in what was then Boston's Jewish quarter. Armed with a little fat Bible, gift of the Reverend Samuel Fox, I had walked the two miles from the YWCA to the Union, and had told the director that I desired to do good. The humor of this statement must have been apparent to him. There before him was a thin, shabbily dressed little woman, with worn shoes, and no gloves, unto whom good most assuredly might have been done, seeking to do unto others what she had not been able to do unto herself. However, the director cordially received my offer and led me at once into a large room furnished with settees occupied by several hundred noisy children. I was given the opportunity to instruct in the Holy Scriptures, and in the ethics of living, twelve smartly dressed, pert-faced little Jewish boys between twelve and fourteen years of age, who had come with the avowed purpose of having fun with the teacher.

The din throughout the room was so great that, had the superintendent used a megaphone, he could not have been heard. My time was mostly spent in dodging the boys, who pulled my clothes, spit at the buttons of my coat, and indulged in other forms of teacher baiting. The fact that for an hour I kept them off the streets was sufficient to make me a useful member of the teaching force. I felt that the street was a fitter place for them to perform. Also, I asked myself what I thought I had to give them anyway. They were better fed and better nourished than I was. What could I do that would interest or instruct them? I found myself unable to answer the question. The urge to do good had been born of the loneliness, incidental to my poverty, that effectively separated me from those whom I would have chosen as friends and comrades. Unconsciously I had sought to realize self-respect by assuming a position of authority toward those who were supposedly worse off than I was. I looked at the motive of my action squarely, and in all honesty, I left the Union hoping never to see that part of the city again.

When it became necessary for me to find work, and when that work led me to the day nursery two blocks from the Union, I was far from joyful. When that experience ended in clubs where I was again expected to keep the young off the streets, I earned my wage in fear and trembling lest the stunts should not succeed in their purpose; in other words, lest the girls would not show up in the club rooms, and I should lose my job.

I now asked myself, was I again about to "do good"? By no means. In my former club experience I had found that neither the girls nor I had ever learned to think. The purpose of our present clubs, then, would be to give us practice in thinking, and to teach us the value of cooperation. With this purpose always before me, I entered upon the first winter in the new clubhouse.

Each club met for two hours, the smaller children from four to six in the afternoons, the older girls from seven to nine in the evenings. The program was similar to that which had been followed in all the library story-hour clubs. The first half hour was given over to business. Important topics were considered, such as promptness, truthfulness, patience, self-control, and a long list of virtues equally desirable. The next half hour was given over to storytelling. Then came a half hour of singing, and a last half hour of folk dancing, which finished the two hours. There were in all nine clubs—one each for fourth, fifth, sixth, and seventh grade children—which met in the afternoons. Other groups for high-school girls, were named—according to the evenings on which they met—Monday, Tuesday, Thursday, Friday, and Saturday Evening Girls.

Many people freely gave their time as group leaders, and the clubs prospered. The girls joyously became acquainted with good literature, good music, and clean sport, and we all learned how to use our minds, and how to think for ourselves.

Those were happy times. Instead of one year, as planned, we remained in the little apartment for seven years. While Edith was working at the pottery on the ground floor, I was working with plans for the clubs on the upper floors and with children in the library at the foot of the street. I say with plans, because my hours at the library did not permit my being with the clubs in person. Therefore I had an assistant who gave all her time to that part of the work.

Never for an instant did I miss the orderly Chestnut Hill house with its lovely garden. Our roof in the North End had many deep boxes filled with earth in which verbenas, heliotrope, and marigolds blossomed; and on neighboring roofs I saw boxes of tomatoes, peppers, and other esteemed vegetables growing. Never for a moment did I miss my low-voiced, well-bred neighbors. My North End friends, with their strident voices, were quite untutored in social graces, but they had an unfailing generosity and a spontaneous gratitude for small attentions, which made one feel warm and comfortable.

I made many friendships with unusual and interesting people. There were the Bs, a laborer and his wife and their seven children, all girls. They occupied four very clean and orderly rooms, and as soon as any one of the seven girls was old enough to go to work, to work she went. I recall that one of the sisters came to me in the library one day and said, "My boss swears something awful, and I don't want to work where it's so uncultured. Could you find me a job?" Of course we could, and we did. Just before her marriage she was in great demand as an interior decorator by some of "Boston's best."

There were the Ps, with four daughters all belonging to our clubs. I shall never forget the day, after a big suburban fire that burned over a hundred-acre district, when the four came marching into the library with small boxes that contained everything they had left in the world. They had barely escaped from their home with their lives and had become separated from one another in the vast crowd that fled before the rushing flames. When I started to commiserate with them, they laughed and said, "You needn't pity us. We're all alive and ready to start over again, but could we sleep at the clubhouse a few nights?"

One of these four girls, "little Annie," enjoyed telling new volunteers about the fire and its results. "It was like this," little Annie would say. "After the big fire we were very poor and I couldn't get a job, so I just sat down on the little built-in couch in the living room at the clubhouse and I told them I wouldn't get off it till they found me a job. I told them they needed a doorkeeper, someone to welcome the girls as they came in, and I just sat and sat, and at last they said that they supposed they would have to have a doorkeeper. Then they built me a little platform and a low desk beside the door. The three dollars I got the first week looked as big as a hundred. I sat at that door all winter, and some days it was pretty cold. Then one day I told them that I thought the girls who worked around there weren't getting proper food at noon, and I wanted to try having lunches for them, cheap and filling meals, you know. I made meals for fifteen cents—spaghetti, coffee, chocolate mould, and things like that—and some days I had as many as twenty girls and they certainly did enjoy themself. I had a grand name," laughed little Annie. "They called me Sunshine."

After the clubhouse was closed, little Annie studied, and studied, and studied till she had to go to the hospital and have an operation on one of her eyes. But what of that? She passed a library examination and became an assistant in one of the branch libraries, where she smilingly charged out books to several hundred children a day.

As we walked together along the street it was a common occurrence for Annie's sleeve to be plucked by some very foreign person who poured out to her a torrent of Yiddish, which later on Annie interpreted to me something as follows, "That was little Hymie's mother, the feeble-minded Hymie, you remember. They didn't want him taken from home"; or, "That was Naomi's sister, the one I used to take every week to the outpatient department"; or, "That was Elsie's husband; he was telling me that just because she came home from the hospital, I shouldn't stop going to see her."

I could fill a book with reminiscences of my friends around Hull Street, not one of whom lives there now. I have watched them emerge with pride and satisfaction. They serve on city committees and on educational boards, and are all for progress. They tell me the clubhouse meant much to them; I tell them it meant more to me.

A short time ago I entered the clubhouse for the first time in the forty years since we left. It has reverted to its former crowded tenement conditions. After all, it served its purpose, and those who used it will never forget it as it was, nor will they forget Mrs. Storrow who provided it.

As a member of the Women's Municipal League[9] and of the North End Improvement Association, I worked with a small group of interested persons to secure a library building for the North End. We were so crowded in the small space we had that lines of waiting children extended out into the street. The room itself was so filled with crowds that no one, young or old, could hope to read quietly.

Through a fortuitous combination of circumstances, we acquired a building at 3a North Bennet Street, with a room for grown-ups, a lecture hall, a children's room, a reference room, and a roof garden. Mayor John F. Fitzgerald[10] had decided that we needed a "bigger, busier, better Boston," and that the people should have a chance to say something about it. To that end, he held town meetings at City Hall for each ward. Anyone could attend, and anyone could suggest an improvement that would make his ward "bigger, busier, and better." The improvements requested by some wards, had they been granted, would have resulted in a "busted, bankrupt, beanless Boston." At our improvement meeting we decided to go to town meeting in a body and one man, the so-called ward boss, was to ask for one thing only, and that was a public library. Now the ward boss was glad to do this, for he knew that the archbishop had a church on his hands to sell, which occupied the very site needed for a library. We knew that the same church dignitary would favor such a sale if approved by the mayor, and he knew that the mayor was interested in giving extended educational privileges to the ward in which he was born.

We went on the appointed night to the dismal old Aldermanic Chamber. Two or three other bodies of citizens from other wards were also there. The mayor entered, took his stand behind the glass water pitcher, pounded the gavel, and the hearing was on. North End came last, and after the others had made requests for school buildings, parks, playgrounds, municipal baths, gymnasiums, community centers, great white ways, fountains, and bandstands, our representative arose and said, "Your honor, we want only one thing, a public library." The silent astonishment of the representatives from other wards, and the gleam of amusement in the mayor's eye, encouraged our speaker to proceed with a vivid description of the need for such an institution in the North End.

Within a year the old church, remodeled as we had planned, was buzzing with activities from cellar to roof, and the librarian was happily writing her report in the sacristy, transformed into the librarian's office.

I had watched the development of the North End with the utmost interest. In 1893, the descendants of the early English residents with few exceptions had migrated before the steady influx of natives of Ireland. The Irish in turn gave place to the Jews. "Solomon Levi" was then the favorite song.[11] At the time the North End Branch Public Library was opened, the Jews were steadily trekking westward, and as they left, the lilting air of "Santa Lucia" was heard on organs drawn through streets and alleys by little horses with gay-colored headdresses, crowned with tinkling bells. The leader of the orchestra had evidently copied his costume from one worn by an Italian opera bandit. The gaily dressed contadina who sang, danced, and jingled a tambourine with the same joyousness at six in the evening that she exhibited at nine in the morning, gave one a thrill of envy. Whenever I heard one of these organs, I would run to the nearest window and, looking on the quaint pair below, with their red-jacketed monkey or green parakeet, I would enter the land of romance. Instead of the drab and utilitarian buildings blotting out the light from our narrow street, I would see terraced gardens rising from the blue waters of the Gulf of Salerno, tier upon tier, till up on the final ridge the trees reared their branches heavy with golden, green, and purple fruit, against a sky blue as the waters of the gulf that mirrored it. This was the setting in which the gay figures belonged. If I, an American who had spent but a few months in Italy, began to sing when the organ ground out Italian airs, it was no wonder that the very laborers in the street kept time to the music with their picks and shovels.

The library's Irish patrons had been insatiable readers of legends and fairy tales; the Jewish readers had loved history, biography, and classical fiction. The gay and temperamental Italians came because they loved the light, the warmth, and the friendliness of the library, but we caught some of them as readers, eventually.

When the new branch was dedicated, the Dante Alighieri Society presented the room for adults with a beautiful bas-relief representing literature and art pouring oil on the flames of knowledge. Above the relief is a bust of Dante, below it the seal of Boston flanked by the wolf of Rome and the fleur-de-lis of Florence.

"The Italians of Boston," said the orator, "desire to be assimilated but *not* absorbed. They do not wish to forget the glories of their motherland, for they believe that, if they cherish the heritage which is theirs by birth in a country which has given to the world such men as Dante and Michelangelo, as Bramante and Garibaldi, they will share with Americans a legacy worth millions, yet which millions could not buy."

The clubs at the library clubhouse had been financed by Mrs. Storrow, but early in 1914 the Saturday Evening Girls' group undertook to furnish the needed funds. Most of the members were now grown-up and at work earning good salaries, and they felt that the time had come for them to show their appreciation to Mrs. Storrow for what she had done. The public library authorities generously granted the use of their basement for club rooms, and Mrs. Storrow had partitions put up and a fireplace built. One of the club members, a young woman with good executive ability, fine character, and poise was chosen as leader of the groups, which remained under my general supervision.

The clubs having been in successful operation in the library basement for a year, Mrs. Storrow, who continued to fund the pottery, decided to move it out of the North End. Edith and I had the pleasant task of finding a suitable location for it. All our Saturday and Sunday afternoons were spent in a search that covered thirteen suburban districts. Amazing adventures attended these efforts. For example, we found an attractive site near the old reservoir in Belmont, a few miles from Boston, made an initial deposit for the land, and in celebration of the event, took a few days' vacation. We had scarcely arrived at our destination when a long-distance telephone message called us back to Boston. The people of Belmont were holding a town meeting in protest against the erection of a "factory," which would fill their quiet town with anarchistic foreign workmen.

We two small women, accompanied by the architects who had drawn plans for the building, and by the lawyer friend who had telephoned us, sat on one side of the hall while over seventy townsmen and women, each one of whom seemed over six feet tall and proportionally broad, sat over on the other side, against us. We heard ourselves described as factory owners who intended to bring to a peaceful neighborhood foreign laborers who might scatter bombs in the street or burn up the town and roast its inhabitants in their beds. Vanquished, but with heads unbowed, we left the meeting. At long last we found a suitable acre of land at the top of Nottinghill Road in Brighton.

The closing of the Hull Street House was a sad affair. Club girls and pottery workers wept continually, both in and out-of-doors. The heavens also wept, and it rained, and rained, and rained. The children brought in, as was their wont, half-drowned kittens found in the burying ground. The Animal Rescue League took them—all but one, a mite no larger than a rat, which drank milk from a medicine dropper with such strength of purpose that we named him Sampson, and took him with us to the little apartment we had rented at the foot of Nottingham Hill. At some remote period of geologic history there had been cast up at this spot a gigantic bubble, which had speedily solidified into a pudding-stone mass. Over this the dust of centuries had drifted until the stone was covered with a carpet of forest grass, shaded by oaks and white birches. There had evidently been a house at some time in this Elysian spot as there was a small orchard of pear trees in full blossom, and one of the largest cherry trees I had ever seen. The lush grass was starred with innocence, cinquefoil, mouse ear, and violets; gray squirrels leaped from limb to limb of the tall oaks; and robins and bluebirds sang in the birch copse.

Ground was broken for the pottery on 16 September 1915. The building was practically completed by 29 November, when the pottery workers assembled for Thanksgiving dinner in the studio. There was at this time a force of twelve Italian and Jewish girls, an English jigger man, two Italian potters, and an Italian who fired the kiln.

The kiln operator was a simple, peaceful soul, who spent his weekdays in the kiln house clad in a dingy pair of overalls and a ragged gray sweater. On Sundays, clean-shaven and neatly garbed in a black coat and striped trousers, beautifully creased, he preached in Italian to crowds of his fellow countrymen in some little hall, or on pleasant days in a public square or vacant lot. He had been converted in Italy and had received a "call to preach." Indeed, he preached every day, and his sonorous voice could often be heard exhorting his fellow workers to let their light shine and to avoid vain babblings.

In a little town on the Gulf of Salerno lived his mother and two sisters whom he was expecting to visit. He had incautiously let it be known that he had saved two hundred dollars for this purpose. Before we left Hull Street he had received several mysterious black-bordered letters stating that some night a "gentleman" would call for this money, and that he had better have it with him if he wished to continue living. He had laughed at these communications and so had we. On going to Brighton, the matter was forgotten, and the Reverend Antonio Santino was given a room in the building, as the loneliness of the site made it desirable to have someone living on the premises.

Shortly after Thanksgiving, at seven in the morning, he appeared at our apartment, disheveled, with tears running down his pale cheeks. His language at best was very broken, but on this particular morning he lapsed so frequently into the Italian dialect of his village that it was some time before we could understand the story he was trying to tell.

He said, "I seet een keel shed weetha Bible when coma pap-pat, soft lika cat. Then door opena leetla crack an beega voice say, deep like drum, 'You geeva me two hund doll or I going keela you.' Then een coma man weetha black mask on a face, peestol een one hand, stilett een other. Theesa man driva me outa keel shed and een house. I say, 'No gotta more nor twanty doll.' 'You geeva me two hund doll or I sure keela you,' say black mask. I say, 'But, I no gotta two hund doll here,' so by an by he say, 'Geeva me the twanty doll an I coma back next time you fira keel for rest.' Then he go, but I no can stay no more."

In confirmation of his story, Reverend Antonio showed us a tiny gash in the table in his room.

"There," he said, "Blacka mask steek his stilett while maka me turn over mattress, opena drawer, looka avery place for fine two hund doll."

Nothing could tempt the man to stay, so Edith and I closed our apartment and went up to the pottery to live. We told the story to the chief of police, who at once assigned a detective to follow up the matter. We were allowed to provide our other workmen with revolvers, and on the nights the kiln was fired, one man continually patrolled the premises while the kiln man went about his work with a gun in his hip pocket.

Weeks and months went by and nothing happened, other than the receipt by Edith of several black-bordered letters written in a Sicilian dialect to the effect that if she ever took back the Reverend S. as a worker, the pottery buildings would be burned to the ground. Years later we discovered that the holdup had been staged by the other Italian employees, to all of whom we had dealt out guns in order that they might protect us. These men had been jealous of a few extra privileges granted to the "preacher" and had gone out to "get him." In 1917, he came back to the pottery and remained until 1925, when he returned to Italy.

With the moving of the pottery to Brighton, the original purpose of giving girls, ambitious for further education, an opportunity to earn by working part-time was abandoned. Indeed, before we had been a year in the North End, we found that pottery making called for the full time of skilled workers. Therefore, when the pottery was established at Nottinghill Road, Edith and I attempted to run it as a regular business; an undertaking for which neither of us was fitted by nature, inclination, or training.

The amount of time we devoted to a study of methods of manufacturing and marketing seems to me now incredible. Our vacation periods for several years were spent in visiting potteries in the United States and in looking up markets for Paul Revere Pottery. In the tile works of Trenton we studied methods of packing saggers and kilns; in the Lenox Potteries[12] we saw how the fine finish of Belleek was obtained; in East Liverpool, Ohio, we wandered through long sheds and watched the production of hotel ware in the Knowles, Taylor, and Knowles Potteries,[13] then said to be the largest in the United States. At the Rookwood studios in Cincinnati,[14] we saw the workers decorating the ware after the manner of old-world craftsmen, absorbed but unhurried. The pottery at Doylestown, Pennsylvania, where Mercer tiles were made,[15] the little shack at Metuchen, New Jersey, where the artist-potter, Charles Volkmar, wrought,[16] and Mrs. Robineau's delightful studio on the hills above Syracuse, New York,[17] are delightful memories.

We made personal attempts to market the ware in Florida during the winter and along the north and south shores of New England in the summer. We learned many useful facts about pottery making and became convinced that the leisurely product of a studio demands rather than provides a steady income.

FOUR

On Loan to Mr. Hoover,

1917–1919

 Until the United States entered World War I, my chief interests had been my library work, the clubs, and the pottery. Now new duties and responsibilities engaged my attention. In April 1917, I put my name on the volunteer list at the Women's City Club of Boston for clerical service. In June I received a call from Mrs. White,[1] the chairman of the War Service Committee, who wanted a food information service planned and started at once. I said I was ready to help, and within an hour Mrs. White appeared and conveyed me in her car to a large empty store on the corner of Bedford and Kingston streets in the wholesale district of Boston. Nothing excepting our first Brookline house ever looked more bare and empty than that enormous room, about one hundred feet long and fifty feet wide.

"This has been offered us, rent-free, for a 'Food Facts Information Bureau,'" said Mrs. White. "What shall we need for furnishings?"

"A desk, several tables, some chairs, two filing cases, and a four-drawer catalog case," I replied.

Two days later these items were installed at the Food Facts Bureau.

By the Fourth of July the bureau was doing a flourishing business. The filing cases contained pamphlets on canning, preserving, and conserving; the catalog drawers were filled with recipes for cake without sugar, omelets without eggs, bread without wheat flour, meat roast without meat, and much material on the mighty power of the bean. Specialists in the crafts of dressmaking, cooking, and all manner of household arts were to be found at the Food Facts Bureau at regular hours ready to give advice and help.

In filing the pamphlets relating to canning, I noted the duplication of effort; for example, I found over eighty pamphlets on the same subject, each treating it from a slightly different angle. I wrote the Food Administration in Washington for a set of their publications, and I wrote again, and yet again, and got no answer; so about the middle of August I asked for a few days leave and went to Washington.

The Food Administration, in August 1917, was located in an apartment hotel on H Street, about as unfitted for office purposes as a rabbit warren. As there were no formalities about entering, I wandered along winding passages, entering room after room filled with women all very busy, about what I could not make out. None of them knew of any publications issued by the Food Administration, other than the Hoover apron patterns.[2] One and all, they declared that it was a Hoover pattern I wanted, and finally one of them insisted on guiding me to the room where these patterns were being distributed. Along with the patterns, I found the documents I sought. As I was going away, well pleased with my pamphlets, I met a friend from Massachusetts who invited me to dinner with a group of women who were to discuss plans for the food-saving campaign, about to be started. Miss Abby Marlatt, head of the economics department of the University of Wisconsin, presided, and after calling on a number of those present, she suddenly turned to me and said, "We'd like a message from Boston." So it came about that I made my first public speech quite unexpectedly. I told what the Women's City Club of Boston was doing and answered questions about our collection of pamphlets. They laughed at my description of the few publications the Food Administration had issued. Evidently Miss Marlatt carried the news of my adventure to Dr. Ray Lyman Wilbur, the president of Leland Stanford University, who was serving as head of the Conservation Division. A few days after my return to Boston I received a telegram as follows: "Would you consider coming to Washington and organizing a Food Facts Library in connection with the Food Administration? State when, for how long, and at what salary."

I replied: "Will arrive Wednesday morning, August 29. Estimate work will take six weeks. No salary. Expenses only."

I applied for a leave of absence and received the approval of my chief at the library for leave WLOP (with loss of pay) for an absence of six weeks.

On arrival in Washington, Wednesday, 29 August, I reported at once to Dr. Wilbur and presented him with a typewritten plan of operation that called for the cooperation of every public library in the country. I also outlined a trip which I considered necessary that would take me to about twenty of the most important libraries in the United States. Dr. Wilbur looked at me quizzically as he considered the plan.

Then he said, "It is a large order. Suppose you talk it over with Miss Barnett, Librarian of the Department of Agriculture, and with Dr. Bowerman, Librarian of the Public Library of the District of Columbia."

I went at once to Agriculture, where Miss Barnett courteously explained that she had an engagement and could not give me the required time. Dr. Bowerman was on a vacation. These facts I reported to Dr. Wilbur, who then said, "Hang up your hat."

I thanked him for the permission, and went to find a place to hang it. For hours I wandered from one office to another; I should say, from one bedroom to another. I finally discovered a small dark room with two windows opening upon a vent. In the middle of the floor stood a telephone. There was nothing else in the room. I wrote my name, large size, on a sign, and stuck it on the door. I then set out on another tour of inspection and found, in a corner of one room, a collection of pamphlets in filing cases in charge of a clerk. This outfit I preempted, and with an air of authority requisitioned two porters to move the filing cases, the pamphlets, one table with typewriter, and two chairs to "my office." I explained to the clerk that she was assigned to the Library Information Service, of which I was chief, and she followed the furniture to my office. On the way I saw two new desks standing in the passage, and told the porters to bring them along with the other furniture. I might add that with this room we inherited a small bathroom. The tub proved a convenient receptacle for duplicate documents. Thus the Food Administration Library Information Service came into being.

By the end of the second week, I was fairly familiar with the organization and had in my office the plan of each of the five floors, with the names of the functions of those occupying the various offices. My business of making the library play a vital part in the organization took me to every department head in turn, as it was necessary to point out to these chiefs the services public libraries could offer as advertising agencies and mediums of approach to the American public.

Before we had been long established, the door of an adjoining room was opened and a voice said, "What are you kids doing in there?"

I explained that we were supposed to be doing library work.

The owner of the voice, who was always known in the Food Administration as Jimmie Collins, said, "Can you be quiet?"

I replied that we could be if we had the opportunity.

He then answered, "I have a little office next this room occupied at present by nothing but filing cases. You can go in if you want to."

We took possession with great satisfaction, and these two offices formed our quarters for the next few months.

On 5 September I started a bulletin, to be called *Food News Notes for Librarians.* The copy was approved by Dr. Wilbur. I soon found that this was the smallest part of the task of getting out a bulletin. It was necessary for the material to have ten OKS. I personally conducted this bulletin from censor to censor till it finally landed in the office of Mr. Hoover's secretary, who looked it over and with a blue pencil cut out all my inspirational material, saying in a perfectly matter-of-fact way, "Guess we'll take out the sob stuff." Mr. Illian, of the art department, performed a remarkable achievement of getting this bulletin through the Government Printing Office in attractive form. The title, "FOOD," on the cover was the first word in display type that I had ever seen printed by that office.

Early in November 1917, I felt the time had come to take the trip I had mentioned to Dr. Wilbur on my arrival, and as a small piece of war service, Mr. Colpitts of Boston made out an itinerary for me which, as to points visited, read as follows: Washington, D.C., to Pittsburgh, Pennsylvania, to Columbus, Ohio, to St. Louis, Missouri, to Kansas City, Missouri, and Kansas City, Kansas, to Denver, Colorado, to Colorado Springs, Colorado, to Salt Lake City, Utah, to Los Angeles, California, to San Francisco, California, to Portland, Oregon, to Seattle, Washington, to Spokane, Washington, to Missoula, Montana, to Minneapolis, Minnesota, to St. Paul, Minnesota, to Chicago, Illinois, to Detroit, Michigan, to Cleveland, Ohio, [and a return to Washington by way of Boston].

I had no sooner set foot in my home city than a friend from the Massachusetts Library Commission grasped me by the hand and said, "There is a meeting out at Newton where they are talking about food conservation. We have just fifteen minutes to get the next train. Hurry up. Can you give the meeting a message?" Yes, I could assure them that we had in Herbert Hoover a leader, who by his supreme trust in the idealism of his fellow citizens had, with a simple appeal to the conscience of America, created an organized army of workers that covered the United States from the Atlantic to the Pacific, from Canada to the Gulf.

I could tell them how in less than a month after the Home Cards had been issued,[3] I had seen them in the homes of cities, towns, villages, and tiny hamlets in twenty-four states: in miners' shacks in Pennsylvania, in cabins on the sandy hills of Utah, and in the forests of the Sierras, in Montana and the Dakotas, in Minnesota and Illinois, in Ohio and Indiana; wherever there were homes, I had seen the food-saving emblems. I could tell them that the instructions on that card were being followed. I could, and did, tell them a few more things. Then I went home to eat a real dinner and to spend a night in my own bed. The next day I left for Washington and was back at my desk three weeks and three days from the time I had left it.

I had been told before leaving Washington that the new building for the Food Administration would be ready about the middle of November, but as the ground had not been broken for the building until October, this had seemed impossible. Great was my surprise, therefore, on finding a very complete and substantial building with all the workers installed as though they had always been there.

My secretary and I were living in a small room near the Hotel Gordon. After four months, spent in the presence of crayon portraits of the family in gilded frames, imitation plants in imitation cut-glass jars, and an imitation radiator which was never known to show any signs of heat, not to mention a bathroom with imitation hot water faucets, we set forth in company with another woman who had been living in like quarters to find an unoccupied barn or garage in which to create a home of our own.

We looked in respectable sections, in distant suburbs, in Negro quarters, and in back alleys where stables appeared to offer possibilities. Finally, on one of the most exclusive residential streets, we found an old tumbledown house that had been single and was now double. One half was occupied by a Negro newsdealer, and the other was untenanted.

The windows were hung with cobwebs, the shutters were falling off, and the door locked as if it were about to fall in, but it was a house. In the front room was a "Latrobe" stove,[4] a heating device that I am willing to recommend without reservations. During one of the coldest winters in the history of Washington, it successfully heated three rooms. A little passage led from the small living room to the dining room, which had a large open fireplace. A second little passage led to the kitchen which opened upon a backyard. Just outside the kitchen door in a small wooden shed was the toilet.

The kitchen had a small sink with hot and cold water faucets and a range connected with a large tank. There was no cellar under the house, and no water except in the kitchen. It was equipped with neither gas nor electricity. Three rooms on the second floor and two on the third floor offered plenty of space, and we almost immediately decided to take it, at a monthly rental of twenty-eight dollars and fifty cents. After it was cleaned up, and the few sticks of furniture lent by various members of the Food Administration were put in place, we found ourselves entirely independent and comparatively comfortable.

The fact that we had to ask our guests to bring their own knives, forks, cups, and saucers when they came to dinner never deterred us from entertaining as many people at a time as the place would hold. We were not dependent upon a landlord for heat, and we always succeeded in the coldest weather in having plenty of coal.

The walls of all the rooms but two were quite bare of paper, and we exercised our individual tastes in painting them. Somebody was always coming home with a can of paint, and as soon as a small space was covered, the other members would gather and say, "I don't see how anybody could have imagined a color so ugly." In the end we had a pink room, a blue room, and several yellow rooms.

Our landlady, daughter of a famous Civil War general, told us that the house was over a hundred years old. The only incident unearthed in connection with the former residents concerned a gentleman from the West Indies who had brought his wife, some forty years ago, to live there. He informed her that she was never to be seen by any person other than himself; therefore, even when she sat at the little front window, she was obliged to wear a little veil.

As finally established, our household numbered five souls: Miss Katharine Wicker, who wrote for the Farm Journal section, Miss Clara Tarbell, who wrote for the women's magazines, Miss Catherine Casassa, secretary to the chief of the Conservation Division, my secretary, Miss Alice Davis, just graduated from Radcliffe, and myself.

Encouraged by our success at homemaking, other women war workers followed our example. The most unique living quarters I visited were aboard an old canal boat near Georgetown. Several enterprising girls occupied this craft, which was partitioned into three rooms, the first a storeroom for provisions, fishnets, and photographic material; the second, a small bedroom with three little beds; and the third, or front room, a living room in which was an airtight coal stove, a blue-flame oil stove, several tables, a desk, bookshelves, and a couch. While the bow of the boat was on land, the stern rested in the water. I had never expected to find such a craft outside the covers of *David Copperfield*, but here it was, and momentarily I expected to see little Em'ly and David emerge from the storeroom, and old Mrs. Gummidge come from behind the stove.

Lack of time prevented us from having our meals regularly at home, though we gave many spaghetti supper parties, the spaghetti being cooked in a large galvanized iron pail hung in the fireplace. There were plenty of eating places in our immediate vicinity where a satisfactory meal could be obtained for sixty cents, and no questions asked when we bundled up the scraps left on our plates and carried them to Priscilla Alden, a cat, once white, who lived with a large family of kittens, still white, in the shed in our backyard.

We had our luncheons at the Food Administration cafeteria, which was so well patronized that I have counted over one hundred and fifty persons waiting in line to get to the counter. In July, during the intensive sugar-saving period, the cafeteria reported that six thousand meals during ten days had been served, and only fifty pounds of sugar had been used for all purposes. This was at the rate of one pound to every one hundred and twenty meals. At the two pounds per month ration, which was in effect at the time, one pound was supposed to go for forty-five meals.

At this time, the Food Administration cafeteria was serving only lunches. Most of the desserts contained such substitutes as honey, maple syrup, or corn syrup. No wheat in any form was served. Bread was made of cornmeal, potato, rice, barley, and corn flour. Beef was served only once a week. The table and cooking refuse amounted to about four ounces per person per day, including fruit and vegetable peelings, plate scrapings, and so forth. This was not waste, because the peelings from potatoes were disposed of for chicken feed. Apple peelings were used for making a juice that served as the foundation for jellies. Other refuse went to the city reduction plant, which was turning out quantities of grease and tankage from which munitions and fertilizers were made. The cafeteria was entirely self-supporting. It was run for the benefit of Food Administration employees to enable them to get a variety of appetizing and substantial food at moderate cost. By using substitutes, food could be served at lower prices, contrary to the widespread belief that substitutes were more expensive.

August descended upon Washington with what seemed the concentrated fire of all previous summers packed into the space of one month. The heat seemed to settle down like a cloud on the thin roofs of our paper buildings and to rise in steaming vapors from the loosely packed bottoms on which the foundations were laid. If we were sufficiently fortunate to finish the day's work at five o'clock, which very seldom happened, there were several comfortable things to do. Twenty minutes by trolley would land us in Georgetown. There, down under the railroad bridge, was a boat house equipped with rowboats and canoes with many gaily colored cushions. Above the bridge were little shops where one could buy sausages, thick slices of bread and butter, pickles, and apples. With this provender we would slowly paddle up the river to a distant spring, and then, shoeless and stockingless, lie down under the great cottonwoods and watch the sun sink behind the low hills of Maryland. When the darkness came, it was time to kindle a brushwood fire, fry the sausages on long sticks, put them between the slabs of bread, and so provide a dish fit for a war worker on the Potomac. The same stick sufficed for baking the apples.

If we were too tired to paddle a canoe, we could take a car to Cabin John bridge. There, a scramble down the bank and over the rocks would bring us to the little green shanty of the ferryman who would row us across the river to the tow path of the canal.

We never tired of watching the big lumbering barges on their way from the Cumberland Mountains to Washington. It was not unusual to see a barge hitched by two ropes to a patient mule plodding onward with a sleepy boy on his back and a little dog frolicking at his heels. At the end of the rope came the slow-moving craft with its off-duty mule staring out of the window of his little stall, its dingy kitten hopefully washing her dusty face, and its human residents, a contented family, placidly sitting under the awning behind the deck house.

Then there was Rock Creek Park, where the drives had been so skillfully planned that the wild woodland character of the place was in nowise destroyed. In the zoo, the deer, the bears, the monkeys, the ostriches, and the gaily plumaged birds seemed to be in their natural habitat. All along the riverbank were stone tables and benches so that one could sit at ease and eat a picnic supper.

As I write, such pictures with their memories, unrecalled for years, come crowding before me, some sharply defined, some vague and nebulous. If, however, all these memories should become blurred, there is one that will remain. I shall always see, as I saw it on my last trip to Arlington, the tapering spire of the Washington Monument, "The Monument" as we call it—white against a steel blue sky, with the crimson oaks in the foreground, and the river, like a curved steel blade, in the middle distance.

Busy as the chiefs were with world problems, the welfare of the Food Administration personnel was not overlooked when the Spanish influenza made its appearances. Each division was visited every morning by someone who took the names of members who were ill. Medical aid was provided, and food was sent from the Food Administration cafeteria so that no one need leave his room until he could do so without danger. When the epidemic showed signs of becoming acute, the experimental kitchen ceased its regular work, baked custards, and made fifty quarts of soup daily. Wives of Food Administration officials either went out nursing or provided care for the sick in their own homes.

During the first week of November 1918, work at the Food Administration was seriously interrupted owing to constantly changing conditions. Plans carefully made for the coming fall and winter were necessarily suspended, and a feeling of unrest and nervousness became apparent. We all rejoiced at the prospect of peace, but for months we had been getting ready for war. The farmers had patriotically produced, the people had as patriotically conserved, and the avenues of trade were shortly to be unblocked all over the world. With the ending of war, the law of supply and demand could again rule. This was a situation difficult to explain, and the difficulty was not lessened by the knowledge on the part of the chiefs that postwar conditions in Europe might call for continued conservation on a wartime basis. Prior to the influenza epidemic, twenty million new home cards had been printed to be released 21 October 1918. All public meetings having been banned because of influenza, the issuance of the cards had been postponed till December first. After the signing of the armistice, the cards were necessarily condemned, but it was decided to carry out the plans made for Conservation Week, which called attention to the sacrifices and needs of our comrades across the sea, and to the practice of thrift, a virtue as necessary to peace as to war. Beyond that week, no plans were made.

The first news of the armistice came on Thursday, 7 November. About noon every whistle in Washington began to blow. Instantly the corridors of our building were filled with excited people reading extras of *The Washington Times*. About one o'clock there was a general exodus to the steps of the Treasury, where we all stood and called for Mr.

McAdoo.[5] Soon a man with a loud voice came up out of the crowd, mounted the platform draped with the American flag, and said: "I call for a committee of five to go and invite the president to come out and talk to us." As the crowd was ready for anything, the committee was speedily formed and dispatched to the White House. Nothing happened, and after singing all the patriotic songs we could think of, we returned to our respective offices. This hilarious meeting made the real announcement on 11 November seem an anticlimax.

On 12 November, the federal food administrators from all parts of the United States met in conference in Washington, and at two o'clock Mr. Hoover delivered an address on the New World Food Situation, his last public utterance before starting for Europe.

In the evening, Food Administration officials had what proved to be their final banquet. The governor of Wisconsin sat at the head of our table.[6] He told of coming to this country from Norway when he was thirteen years of age. He had practiced food conservation from the start, as he had been shipwrecked on his way to America. When he was picked up on Anticosti Island and carried to the mainland, he weighed forty-eight pounds. He said that he had always wanted to go to college, and that by studying at all kinds of odd times, he had fitted himself to enter the University of Wisconsin. When he first read about "commencement" exercises, he thought that this referred to the beginning of the school year, and as a consequence, he went to register in June instead of September. In 1913, when he went back to Norway on a visit, he traveled on one of his own company's ships. Since then, he said, he had sold out everything and given his whole time to war service, to give back in a slight measure some of the things that this country had given to him.

The thirteenth and last issue of *Food News Notes* was on the press when it became known to the chiefs that the armistice was about to be proclaimed. It was, therefore, suggested that the issue of ten thousand copies be scrapped. I protested, as almost the entire bulletin was devoted to articles on the elimination of waste, and the destruction of the bulletins would be a very wasteful performance. My protest was heard and the bulletins were sent out as usual.

It was the first of January before I finished the work incidental to the thrift program, which had been given to thousands of libraries, north, south, east, and west. By that time the Food Administration office building was almost deserted. As for our little house, Miss Wicker and I were the only ones left. She had been borrowed by the Treasury Department, and I had remained, with a few others, to gather up loose ends and to collect and assemble valuable data, which would otherwise have been thrown away.

During my sixteen months as a Food Administration worker, I had had the opportunity and privilege of visiting many of the government departments and offices and had become acquainted with the men and women known as Uncle Sam's clerks, who file letters, reports, memoranda, and documents; who keep accounts and make surveys; who do valuable work, and who prepare copy for publications that describe the function and works of the federal government. Before going to Washington, I had known nothing about the executive branch of the government; and even after I had been there some months I wondered what the vast company of men and women who poured out of the government offices at four-thirty every afternoon found to do. When I learned, I made a vow, after the manner of that good old Methodist, the Reverend Samuel Fox, that I would tell the world about my discovery.

One evening when my work at the Food Administration office was finished, I went home and told Miss Wicker about this vow.

"What do you plan to do?" she asked.

"I'll tell you tomorrow," I said, and ran up the little steep stairs to my room.

I can think more easily with a pad and a pencil. As a heading I write, "Purpose"—"Expected Results." Sometimes I cover many sheets of paper with hundreds of words, which eventually reduce themselves to several sentences. When I had been writing for some time, but before I had come to the several sentences stage, I sought the chief of the Information Division, who, like a few of the rest of us, had lingered on. I found him alone in a perfect welter of papers, posters, pamphlets, press releases, photographs, and telegrams.

"Mr. Allen,"[7] I said, "I have always believed that this is the greatest government in the world, but I never knew why. Now I know, and I want to tell the world about it."

I was serious, and he respected my mood.

"There's nothing like the printed word," he said, being a journalist, "but your idea has no news value, so you can't get it into the papers, and the government does not believe in advertising."

Here he rested his head on his hand and became silent. After a few moments of this prayerful attitude he looked up, tilted his chair back, put his hands behind his head, and said, "The government is damned strong on education. You must get across the idea that this is education. Draft a plan for a series of bulletins, do one complete, and I'll see the secretary of the interior about getting the Bureau of Education to sponsor it."

"I'll do it at once," I said and ran all the way home.

"Come along, Wicker," I cried, "I'll pay for a dinner at the Fife and Drum and tell you my plan."

That night I began to put the plan on paper. It was a very simple one: a small government news sheet entitled *National Library Service* was to go monthly to the eight thousand libraries to which *Food* had been sent. I prepared a dummy of the first one and submitted it to Mr. Allen.

"It's good," he remarked, and picked up the telephone.

"Interior," he said. Then, "Secretary's Office." Then, "Hello, Cotter, this is Allen. Can I see the secretary? Thanks, be over in five minutes."

He hung up, grabbed his hat, and strode out of the office. In a half hour he was back.

"The secretary says you'd better see Pettijohn of the Educational Extension Division at the Bureau of Education," he said. "Keep your eyes on the ball, and you'll win; go to it." He patted me on the back encouragingly, and I went to find Dr. Pettijohn.

Dr. Pettijohn was in peacetime the director of educational extension work at the University of Indiana. In wartime, he was the director of the Americanization work of the Bureau of Education, and my idea appealed to him.

"Suppose you put the bulletin into shape for the printer," he said. "Claxton (commissioner of education)[8] is sure to approve it if the secretary is favorable, and he can get the War Fund."

I had written the text for many bulletins, but I had never prepared a bulletin for the printer, and there was no one whom I could consult, so I got a style book from the Government Printing Office and gave, as I thought, a pleasing variety to the headings and subheadings of the reading matter by using as many different styles of types as I could find. I gave the bulletin the title *National Library Service* and marked it Vol. 1, No. 1.

By what means Dr. Pettijohn obtained the secretary's OK I never knew; nor did I ask; nor did it occur to me that it was not my business to take the copy personally to the Government Printing Office. Indeed, I thought it was my business, and in less than a half hour after I had received the accepted copy, I handed it personally to the clerk in the Printing Office, whom I had already met in connection with the printing of *Food News Notes*.

I told him I hoped it would go right along, so he marked it "Rush," and started it on the road to the presses. Now the Government Printing Office is accustomed to follow a layout with absolute fidelity, and it did not deviate from this practice in printing my bulletin, which had the effect of making real printers outside the Government Printing Office laugh, and take it humorously, or all but shed tears, and take it sadly.

The leading editorial, with the caption "Problems of Readjustment," was signed by J. H. Pettijohn, Director, Division of Educational Extension. This editorial was followed by notes on the services offered by government departments and organizations. The bulletin further stated that the office from which it was issued would serve as a clearing house for information between the government and public libraries.

Dr. Pettijohn had told me that he would find me a room in which to work in the Interior Department. Every day I went to the building to inquire about it, and every day he said, "Tomorrow." In the meantime I worked in the all-but-abandoned Food Administration Building preparing copy for *National Library Service*, Vol. 1, No. 2.

About the middle of January, I was told that the files containing much information which would be useful in the new office would be sent to the Library of Congress if I did not get a room at the Interior immediately. Dr. Pettijohn told me he had tried in vain, day after day, to find a room and had about given up. I asked him if he had any objection to my trying. "Certainly not," he replied, so I went directly to the office of Senator Henry Cabot Lodge of Massachusetts and had a talk with the great man himself. What report I made, I cannot recall, but he evidently got the idea that a Massachusetts woman was not being treated with the consideration due a citizen of that state, so he wrote a letter to the secretary of the Interior that burst all barriers and resulted in my assistant and myself, with all our filing cases, being moved forthwith to a large, clean, sunny office a few doors from the secretary's suite. Letters began to pour in from all parts of the United States, and we were soon almost as busy as in the days before the armistice.

We had hoped that the Library Information Service would become a permanent section of the Bureau of Education, but in June our hopes died. The commissioner of education had had many projects under consideration long before the library service idea was suggested. However, he generously said that if I would finish the series of articles on the federal government that had been running in the bulletin, he would have them printed in book form. This I estimated would take three months, so I asked and obtained from the Boston Public Library some more leave WLOP.

I told Miss Wicker that I intended this book to be my little monument.

"O, come," she said, "you don't intend to let all this work end with one little book, do you?"

"Well, I can't put up any more funds," I replied, "and I can't afford to lose my job in Boston. I must get back to work."

Miss Wicker then said, "I suppose you've observed that whenever the government needs money for something, somebody introduces a bill. Why don't you introduce a bill?"

"Who am I that I should do this thing?" I gasped.

"Well, of course, it is a drawback that you aren't anybody," she agreed, "but perhaps you can make some higher-up librarian or congressman believe that the idea is his."

The next morning I went to the office of Mr. Glass, the chief of the Division of Publications of the Interior department, and asked if I could see a bill.

"House or Senate," said he.

"House," I replied.

"On what subject," said he.

"Education," I replied.

I had learned that if one wishes to secure action, one must be definite and direct; hesitation leads to suspicion; and suspicion leads to investigating by experts not necessarily expert on the subject under consideration.

Mr. Glass presented me with a bill introduced by Mr. Raker of California,[9] which had to do with correspondence courses. As I took the bill in my hand, I experienced a distinct thrill. The government about which I was so enthusiastic had been created by acts of Congress that had first appeared as bills. I was on the verge of another great discovery. I had learned superficially how the government, as represented by the executive departments, worked; now I was to learn how Congress worked.

"May I take this bill to my office?" I asked humbly.

"Certainly," replied Mr. Glass. "You needn't return it; I have plenty of copies."

I still have that bill, as it was my introduction to an adventure in legislation that extended over a period of nine years, and that cost me in traveling expenses, hotel bills, and clerical service an amount representing more than a year's salary. The education I bought for that price I would not exchange for double the amount.

It was the month of June when I received from Mr. Glass the much-prized bill. I took it home to Miss Wicker, who said, "You told me there was some sort of a library meeting at Asbury Park next week; why don't you go to it and get some of the big city librarians to propose this plan? Then get a congressman to introduce a bill about it."

"I will," I replied, and ran upstairs to my room to write a bill, using Mr. Raker's as a model.

At the library meeting I explained my plan to ten well-known librarians. They were pleased with the idea of a national service that would keep libraries informed about the new publications issued by Uncle Sam and about old ones, which were in many cases of equal value and interest. All signed their names in approval of the project, and I hurried back to Washington. From the train I went directly to Mr. Raker's office.

I could see the member from California sitting alone in his inner office, but when his secretary said, "Go right in," I could not believe my ears. Were there no formalities? Did she understand that I was not a California friend of a friend of a friend of the congressman? She laughed and said, "Go ahead in." So in I walked and told that open-hearted, sympathetic Californian all about the plan, and asked him to introduce our bill.

"Why, of course, I will," he said. He took my draft in his hand, called for his secretary, and dictated the text of the bill as it finally appeared. When his secretary had transcribed it, he said, "We should add a paragraph asking for an appropriation. How many people will be needed to carry on the office?"

"Six," I replied.

"What for?" he said.

I explained in detail. He then took a ponderous statute book from the shelves, turned the leaves till he found what he wanted, gave titles and salaries to the six, and the bill was, as he said, "drafted." It went posthaste to the Government Printing Office and was in the House in printed form in time to be read by the clerk at the afternoon session. I had never felt so powerful as when I exhibited the printed bill to Miss Wicker that evening.

The next day I showed it to Mr. Glass, who read it aloud:

A BILL To provide for a library information service in the Bureau of Education.

Be it enacted by the Senate and House of Representatives of the United States of America in Congress assembled, That there is hereby created in the Bureau of Education a service to be called the Division of Library Service, which shall be under the charge of a director, who shall be appointed by the Secretary of the Interior and who shall receive a salary of $4,000 per annum. There shall also be appointed by the Secretary of the Interior the following assistants and their employees at the salaries designated: One assistant director, at $2,500 per annum; one chief clerk, at $2,000 per annum; one stenographer, at $1,000 per annum; one messenger, at $800 per annum; and in addition thereto such other employees as the Secretary of the Interior shall deem necessary; Provided, That not more than $8,100 annually shall be expended for salaries of experts, assistants, and employees outside the District of Columbia and for travel, stationery, printing, and binding, unless previously authorized by law. It shall be the purpose and duty of such division to increase the efficiency of American libraries by providing current information concerning government activities. It shall collect and organize information regarding printed matter issued by the Federal Government, and shall make available to the libraries of the United States the sources of such information. It shall provide digests of this material, with suggestions as to its use, in order that such material may be made quickly available to users of libraries.

The Secretary of the Interior is authorized to make all necessary rules and regulations for carrying out the purpose of this act.

In due course the bill was favorably reported by the House Committee, Representative Dallinger writing the report,[10] and by the Senate Committee, Senator Walsh writing the report.[11] A few days later it was laid aside in the House by motion of Representative Blanton of Texas,[12] and in the Senate by motion of Senator Smoot of Utah.[13] Every time thereafter that the bill came up, it was laid aside by motion of these two men. I learned, to my profound amazement, that *one* dissenting vote in either house could kill a bill.

The two hearings accomplished, I sat down in the living room with Miss Wicker and told her I was going home the next morning. Till long after midnight we sat and reviewed the astounding events in which she, a poorly paid small-town Virginia schoolmarm, and I, a poorly paid and obscure library worker, had taken part. "We shall never be the same again," she said.

The next day I said good-bye to my friends in the Interior department. Secretary Lane said, "Not good-bye, au revoir," and presented me with an autographed copy of *The American Spirit*.[14]

My faithful and efficient secretary, who had been taken into the chief clerk's office, was to guide through the Government Printing Office my book, which was entitled *The Federal Executive Departments as Sources of Information for Libraries*. One of the most interesting jobs in connection with compiling this material had been the obtaining of prefatory letters signed by secretaries of the executive departments. Knowing that these busy men would, in all probability, not take time to write letters themselves, I imitated as nearly as possible the style of each one and sent the letters around to their offices for approval and for their handwritten signatures. Some of the officials signed them as they were, others changed them, and a few completely rewrote them. Secretary Baker, of War,[15] Assistant Secretary Franklin D. Roosevelt, of the Navy—later on president of the United States—and Secretary Redfield, of Commerce,[16] gave me appointments, and with them I talked personally. Assistant Secretary Roosevelt sat down beside me on a great leather sofa and chatted informally. He was an enthusiastic believer in the plan for a library information service. Secretary Baker dictated rapidly his own letter, while I waited, and signed it as rapidly in a delicate, almost feminine hand. Secretary Redfield came in five minutes later than the time he had set for my appointment. He apologized most graciously for having kept me waiting, and then proceeded to show me some of the latest experiments of the Bureau of Standards, among them several pairs of very smart shoes made of fish skin. Before I knew it I was telling him all about the Paul Revere Pottery and some of the troubles we had experienced.

"Next time Bleininger, our chemical expert, is up your way, I'll have him look in on you," said the secretary, and true to his word, he did, with the result that Mr. Bleininger gave Edith some valuable advice.

The entire book was to be prefaced by President Wilson. Secretary Lane himself sent my suggested preface to the president for his approval and signature. The president made only one change in the copy. I had headed it "To the Librarians of the United States." He crossed off "of the United States" and made the copy read "To the Librarians." With the ideal before him of a league that would take in the nations of the world, he could not address merely the librarians of the United States. His desire was to address the librarians of the world.

My leave of six weeks granted in August 1917 had extended into one hundred and four weeks when, on Monday, September 8, I reported for work at the Boston Public Library. From that date until June 1928 I continued to peg away at odd times at the piece of legislation which sat on my shoulders like the old man of the sea, and which seemed at times as if it would strangle me.

I used my vacations in writing articles on the value of government publications, in giving talks at library and other educational meetings, and in going to Washington in the interests of the bill.

When President Wilson's term was over and the Sixty-sixth Congress came to an end, the bill died. It was reintroduced in the Sixty-seventh, and again was automatically laid aside every time it came up, on the motions of the senator from Utah and the representative from Texas.

On one of my fruitless trips to Washington, I had occasion to visit an office in the Department of Commerce. While turning over the leaves of a Bureau of Standards publication, the thought came to me that I was in the same building with the man who had been chief of the Food Administration. I asked for a brief appointment, got it, and was soon sitting beside Mr. Hoover's desk telling about the bill and the seeming impossibility of getting any action on it. Mr. Hoover listened intently to my exposition, and gave his opinion without hesitation.

"General Dawes is the man to advise you.[17] I will see that you get an appointment with him." I thanked him and went back to the outer office, while one of the assistants telephoned the Bureau of the Budget of which General Dawes was then the director.

General Dawes, having heard my statement, said, "Have you seen Carter?"

"Many times," I replied.

"Go see him again," said the general. "This piece of work should be done in the Government Printing Office." I did not attempt to explain to the general that the librarians felt that the office should be in the Bureau of Education. I had asked his advice and he had given it. I thanked him and went at once to the Government Printing Office where I had a long conference with Mr. Carter, the government printer. The result of this conference I reported in the following note to one of the library magazines:

The need for a Central Information Office for libraries was never greater than it is at the present time; but I have been informed by those in authority that during the period of reorganization no new government divisions will be approved. I have also been informed by the Public Printer that he is so thoroughly convinced of the need for the suggested service that he proposes to start it in the office of the Superintendent of Documents without legislative action, as he believes it to be a legitimate service for that office to perform.

The librarians have for years been urging the establishment of a library information office, and they have gone on record time after time, requesting that it be placed in the Bureau of Education, where as an educational extension service they believe it belongs.

Now that it is decided to place it in the Government Printing Office, the only position librarians can reasonably take is one of thankfulness that it is to be, rather than of regret that it is not to be where they had hoped.

Two years passed without perceptible action on the part of the Government Printer, so, to stir things up a bit, the bill was again introduced in the House of Representatives of the Sixty-eighth Congress, the only change being slight increases in the salaries suggested. On 30 January 1924, Honorable Frederick W. Dallinger, chairman of the House Committee on Education, called a hearing at which statements in favor of the bill were made by representatives of several library organizations, by the secretary of the National Education Association, and the commissioner of education. At noon the Committee went into executive session and at half past twelve the bill was favorably reported.

I returned to Boston and began the task of getting signatures to a petition addressed to the chairman of the Senate Committee on Education,[18] worded as follows: "We respectfully urge your consideration of S3557, a bill to provide for a library information service in the Bureau of Education. If it is not desirable to report this bill favorably without having further information on it, may we request that you hold a hearing upon it as soon as possible." When the petition had been signed by some thousand librarians and educational leaders, I carried it to Washington and handed it to the chairman. He glanced at it casually, gave me an inscrutable look, signified that with the delivery of the paper into his hands I need give it no further thought, and began turning over the papers on his desk as though I were no longer present.

Even though he was a senator and a great man, I did not consider his manners worth reproducing, so I thanked him most cordially for his kindness in giving me a personal interview. As he did not appear to hear me, I bade him good-day, and went out with a jaunty air and a condescending smile for the clerks in the outer office. The sixty-eighth session of Congress closed without a hearing before the Senate Committee, and S3557 and HR633 were buried along with thousands of other reported and unreported bills.

In January 1928, after consulting with the superintendent of documents, I prepared to reintroduce the bill with one important change in the wording. Instead of specifying that the office should be located in the Bureau of Education, we specified the Government Printing Office. Senator Moses of New Hampshire[19] was at this time chairman of the Joint Committee on Printing, so I went down to Washington to ask if he would sponsor the bill. He read it, handed it back, and said, "No, I'm against the creation of any more bureaus. See Wold, and find out what can be done about this by the superintendent of documents without legislation."

Now Mr. Wold, who was the secretary of the Joint Committee on Printing, occupied a cavelike room in the Capitol located near that part of the cellarage known as "under the dome." He listened cheerfully to my story and complimented me on the idea. Then he pointed to some great rolls of galley proof on a long table and said, "I'm getting out a biographical dictionary that will contain sketches of every congressman who ever served, and I'm having a lot of trouble getting information about some of them. Suppose you could help me with the New England men?"

"Of course," said I, welcoming this chance to do a favor for one who could do so much for the libraries if he would.

He then handed me a bundle of yellow and pink slips and promised to send others. I said no more at that time about "The Library Information Service."

Thenceforth, instead of preparing publicity on the bill, I toiled over biographies of our congressmen, searched the files of old town newspapers, dug into vital records, and had interviews with great-grandnephews, or intimate friends of the descendants of some man named Smith, who died a hundred years ago and apparently never got his name into the *Congressional Journal* of his day, excepting when he took his seat. Sometimes these men, according to different newspapers, died on several different dates. About one of them I wrote a village school superintendent and asked if he would send a boy at my expense to the graveyard to copy from the gravestone the date of the congressman's demise. The superintendent replied that as the snow was very deep and the graveyard in a lonely place, he had himself gone and scraped the snow from the stone only to find the date obliterated.

Mr. Wold testified his appreciation of my efforts by flooding me with pink and yellow slips, and I continued to labor with them until I felt I had earned the right to call his attention to my own project. I therefore prepared and had printed a four-page leaflet that contained the titles of government publications issued the previous week, with brief digests of their contents. In March 1928, I gave copies of this leaflet to Mr. Wold with a suggestion that the Government Printing Office should issue a weekly list similar to the one I had prepared. I said nothing about the library information office as I felt that one step at a time was all we could expect, and that if the weekly list increased the sale of government publications, the information service might be given consideration.

Mr. Wold read the bulletin and responded with the prescribed formula known as "passing the buck." In other words, I was told to see someone else. This time it was the superintendent of documents. I thanked him and went at once to the dingy little basement office of the building occupied by that official. After spelling my name three or four times and finally writing it on a paper, the doorkeeper telephoned the superintendent's office. Too tired with this effort to speak, he nodded his head, and I entered the elevator, which waited a few moments to get its breath, and then began to crawl up past floor after floor equipped with the dry and inflammable wooden shelving on which the publications of the United States government were stored.

When I reached the office of the superintendent of documents he was out, so I began to examine the latest publications, which were piled on a table. After a few minutes he entered in his shirtsleeves, grabbed his office coat, stuck his arms into the sleeves, and gave me a handshake that, for the moment, deprived me of the power of speech. I presented him with my leaflet, which he wholeheartedly commended, and which he said he would show to the government printer. There seemed to be nothing more for me to do, so I returned to Boston.

In June, I stopped off in Washington on my way to the annual meeting of the American Library Association in West Baden, Indiana, and called on Mr. Wold who was most affable and as noncommittal as a guilty person on trial for murder. I saw also the superintendent of documents and the government printer, who said they were considering the matter, a statement that had no news value as I had heard it for nine years.

As I left the Government Printing Office, my thoughts flew back to that June day in 1919 when I had so joyously hurried home bearing the firstborn of a family of bills for the establishment of a library information service. I realized that I had learned enough about the way Congress works to pay for all my trouble, but my heart was heavy over my utter failure to bring about the public service I had envisioned with such enthusiasm.

Before leaving for West Baden, I wrote appreciative letters to Mr. Wold, to Mr. Tisdel, superintendent of documents, and to other officials whom I had seen in the interests of the bill. Just one week later, as I was leaving the breakfast room in the West Baden hotel, I received a telegram which read: "First issue of the Weekly List will appear about July first. Signed, Tisdel."

The adventure, known among my friends as my congressional tilt, was over. The results differed from those of other tournaments in that no one was unseated and no one's feelings were injured.

FIVE

A Civil Servant,

1919–1945

 On my return from Washington, my place at the North End Library having been filled, I was given the title of supervisor of circulation with instructions to coordinate the work of the various departments of the main library; no instructions as to how the coordination was to be effected were given. Though this proved to be what Dr. Wilbur would have called "a large order," I was not discouraged. It was a "message to Garcia."[1] To get busy on something definite while I found out what was to be coordinated, I suggested that the public stenographer, who occupied, rent-free, a fair-sized room on the corridor at the front of the library, should move to a smaller room and that her room should become an information office. In this room I installed a selection of reference materials and about a thousand government publications, an innovation that was commended by the Honorable Calvin Coolidge, then governor of Massachusetts and later president of the United States, who wrote the director of the library as follows:

> The Commonwealth of Massachusetts
> Executive Department,
> State House, Boston
> 1st December, 1919

Mr. Charles F. D. Belden,
Public Library,
Boston, Mass.
Dear Mr. Belden:
    You are to be most heartily congratulated upon the public spirited action you have taken in preparing for an up-to-date Govern-

ment News Service in the Boston Public Library. It is to be sincerely hoped that Congress can at an early date pass the measure empowering the Interior Department, through the Bureau of Education, to establish an office which will make it possible to open this Service to the public.

The stability of our Government depends on the loyalty of the citizens of the United States who are—in the final analysis—the Government. Nothing will ensure that loyalty more effectively than a knowledge of the functions and actions of that Government which libraries above all institutions are qualified to make clear to the people.

Very truly yours,
Calvin Coolidge

In a very short time two rooms adjoining the Information Office were added to it.

Being a newcomer in the Central Library, I decided to devote myself to building up the circulation in the branch libraries. Mr. Langdon Ward, the supervisor of branches and my immediate chief, was a literary man of a type fast vanishing. He was a genuine book lover who had as much liking for office routine as a Charles Lamb, an Oliver Goldsmith, or a Samuel Johnson.

He occupied a tiny office piled high with dusty records, maps, book recommendation cards, and books. Every pigeonhole of his black walnut rolltop desk was bursting with papers, dusty and ink-spattered. I can see him now sitting placidly before this mass of materials, which he had scrupulously saved, talking in the most sympathetic and almost affectionate way about one of his branch workers who was ill and who should have a six months' leave, or chatting amiably about some work of philosophy or book of poems that had particularly appealed to him. His librarians were genuinely fond of this chief in whom there was no guile. They loved to see him come plodding into a branch library in the stout rubbers he usually wore, his head bent forward, his green cloth bag clutched under one arm, and his big unwieldy umbrella under the other. He seldom made a tour of inspection, but instead he sat down beside the librarian and gave a pleasant dissertation on interesting articles he had been reading in current periodicals, or on old books with which he was renewing acquaintance. His favorite humorist was Artemus Ward. "Not," he was wont to remark, "a relative so far as I know."

Mr. Ward did not see much sense in my endeavor to study the character of the circulation, to speed up the processing of new books, and to establish a uniform code of operation for all branches. However, he tolerated the actions of one of his former branch librarians and his former branch librarian tried, as far as possible, to abstain from suggestions of up-to-date methods, which brought to his face a look of pained surprise as if he had unwittingly nourished a viper in his bosom.

This new work, though interesting, was decidedly strenuous, so, not having had any real vacation since the summer of 1917, I decided in 1922 to spend several weeks in Europe. Edith Brown and I pooled our assets and found we had sufficient, if we traveled economically, to see something of France, Belgium, and England. We sailed, therefore, on the seventeenth of June, for Le Havre. I had an approval from *The Christian Science Monitor* for articles on foreign libraries, which furnished me with a definite subject on which to write. Edith had also her program for visiting potteries.

Having heard of the difficulties of getting information about methods of procedure in foreign libraries, I had provided myself with several letters of introduction from Mr. Hoover, Senator Lodge, and the director of the Boston Public Library. With the exception of the Bibliothèque Nationale in Paris, I entered libraries and received utmost courtesy without showing my letters. As soon as I explained that I worked in the Boston Public Library, they said that no other introduction was necessary.

At the Bibliothèque Nationale all was different. I had no sooner passed through the gateway leading to the court than the concierge called from his lodge just inside the gate, "La carte! La carte!" I promptly handed him one of my notes of introduction. He perused it with a care that demonstrated that he could not read a word of it, and returned it with a polite bow. Pointing to a door across the court he said economically, "A gauche."

Proceeding "à gauche" through several long corridors, I arrived at a sort of ticket office wherein sat a very delightful old person reading a huge folio volume. Without looking up he silently extended his hand for "la carte." This he read and laid aside. He then scribbled something on a red card which he held out for me, still without raising his eyes. I accepted the red card, but not feeling quite safe without my letter, said humbly, "La carte?"

"I will keep it," said the old gentleman in perfectly good English, his eyes still bent on his folio.

My ancestors had won their name of "warrior" on French battlefields. Yet, as I traveled through France and Belgium and looked upon miles of rubbish heaped on the torn, gashed earth, where but a few short years ago charming villages and well-cultivated farms fenced with tidy hedgerows had been, I felt that all my future fights would be against wars, which exchange order for disorder, and beauty for ugliness at a cost of millions of lives. Should I ever waver in this resolve, all I need to do is to remember Ypres as I saw it on a gray and sunless day in August 1922.

Opposite the station, as if to hearten the visitor, a garden had been laid out, and for a few squares new buildings rose here and there. "Not so bad," I said, and then we entered the Grande Place where the ruins of the fine old thirteenth-century buildings had not as yet been leveled, and where on shattered pillars and crumbling walls hung evergreen wreaths and small cotton flags. In the midst of this tragic place a fair was in process. "Come and have your fortune told," I read on a sign, as if to say, "The past is past; the future is all before us."

On a bandstand in the center of the square stood an armless man who was selling postal cards from a tray supported by a strap around his neck. In front of the ruins of the cathedral was a booth, the back draped with a Belgian flag, before which was placed a gleaming white statuette of Christ on the cross. This square was one of the saddest sights I have ever seen—the crumbling ruins, the fair in progress in their midst, the sad-faced Christ on his cross, and a great, silent stream of black-clothed people ever flowing toward the graves of their dead.

We joined the processions, and with different groups visited many of the cemeteries. Incongruous as it may seem, these were among the more cheerful sights. The plain little crosses stood in tidy rows in the midst of flower beds where sweet williams, poppies, lupines, marigolds, and roses grew in spendthrift profusion. The grass plots between the beds were neatly trimmed, and above all the larks were singing.

All day long I saw no one smile, save a woman in the little front yard of a very new green cottage surrounded by a white iron fence, half-covered with scarlet runners. She had just put her baby into a little wicker creeper, and as he began jumping it across the yard, she clapped her hands and laughed aloud.

We walked through street after street of corrugated iron sheds, which served as dwelling places for houseless families. Many other long streets had only the cobblestones intact, with not a sign of a building. One of these trails ended in a jungle of tangled wire and broken bricks, from which rose the corner of a building with outlines of windows. Beyond, stretching away for miles to the horizon, was the bare, shell-torn plain. Over all, the clouds hung low like a curtain about to fall, while a mournful wind sighed among the rank weeds and over the mounds of unsightly rubbish.

From Ypres we went to Ostend, where we boarded the channel boat for Dover. As the train for London traversed green meadows dotted with grazing cattle, as it ran between low hills where flocks of sheep were grazing, as it passed mile after mile of carefully nurtured gardens, the war-torn fields and woods of France and Belgium assumed the aspect of a dream. When, late in the evening, we drove through the brightly lighted streets of London, I experienced a sense of safety I had not known since I landed on the dock at Le Havre.

With the exception of delightful hours spent in the British Museum and in various London libraries, my pleasantest memories are of Oxford. A lasting impression of this quiet town is one of peace and order, under the influence of which rare achievement is possible without hurry or commotion. The very turf appears to produce its close-clipped carpet by itself. The garden borders, the well-trimmed hedges, the neatly swept walks, all look as if they have been thus from the beginning; and the blackened stones of the buildings, the weather-beaten statues and reliefs, which have withstood the suns and storms of centuries, add to this effect.

In all the colleges we visited were tablets bearing long lists of the names of those who had given their lives in the world war. I could never get these boys out of my mind as we walked in the quadrangles of the ancient colleges where they must so many times have strolled of an evening, pipe in mouth and hands in pockets.

Through Warwick and Stratford, and then to the "Five Towns," and on to the Lake District we journeyed. Late in August 1922 we sailed for home. Shortly after my arrival in Boston, one of the branch librarians telephoned that our good friend, Mr. Ward, the supervisor of Branch Libraries, had died very suddenly the week before! An unexpected result of this sad happening was my appointment as his successor.

Having met with the thirty or more branch librarians as one of their number for more than twenty years, I feared it would not be an easy matter to be their supervisor. However, I interpreted the task to be the gathering together of many individual ideas and of finding among them the common denominator of action. From the beginning my comrades made the task easy and pleasant.

As chief of a rather influential professional organization, many duties came to me, such as serving on committees of civic and educational organizations. My connection with the American Library Association took me to many different states. On one of these trips to the Pacific coast I stopped for a day at Kendall, Kansas. About this day I wrote a friend as follows:

Had I not faithfully promised to write of my Kendall adventures, the story of that town, so far as I am concerned, would remain unwritten for the reason that there is nothing interesting to write. All the picturesqueness is gone and only squalor and apparent impotence remain. To write about it is like trying to tell the story of a happy tea party from the resulting garbage.

At 5 A.M. on June 16th in the Year of Grace, 1936, I was wakened as the train jolted to a stop at a water tank. Over the prairies of Kansas the sun was slowly rising in a cloudless sky. Groves of cottonwoods relieved to a certain extent the monotony of the landscape. I say "to a certain extent" advisedly, for of all trees the cottonwood seems the most ungraceful. No poet would ever write about anything that stood beneath a spreading cotton-wood tree.

The little towns sprawl over the face of the prairie, their ugliness shown up in strong sunlight. They are plainly more prosperous than they were fifty years ago. Now dumps are for worn out automobiles, then they were for buffalo and cattle bones. Nowhere did I see a good old democrat wagon. As for horses I began to believe they were extinct in this part of the country till I saw three bony specimens grazing on the prairie.

Good roads have taken the place of dusty trails, electric lights and faucets have ousted kerosene lamps and pumps, telephones and radios are in most homes. Yet notwithstanding these great improve-ments the towns are indescribably unattractive. Why? I asked myself again and again. Because the roofs have no overhang and the houses are so nearly square in outline? Because house doors, win-dows, and all trim are the same dull drab color? It is something deeper than that. The people who built these shelters, I will not call them homes, have no thought nor care for order and beauty.

Between towns I feasted my eyes on the lovely flowers of the plains; yellow prickly pear cacti, sunflowers, gaillardia, wild squash, yellow roses and blue vetch, white thistles, primroses and soap weed, deep magenta Indian bread root, and numerous other familiar blossoms whose names I do not recall. Oh, yes, and loco, which still intoxicates the cattle.

At Lakin, Kansas, I left the train and was met by a hale old gentleman who proclaimed himself Mr. Hammond, President of the Hamilton County Historical Association. He escorted me to a model T Ford painted light blue.

First we called on Mrs. India Simmons, known as the historian of southwestern Kansas. Mrs. Simmons had little to contribute beyond the fact, familiar to me, that there had been in 1885 a county-seat fight which ruined the town of Kendall. All the persons whose names were on my list had died and most of their descendants had trekked to parts unknown.

After a pleasant half hour with the "Historian of southwestern Kansas" we started for the eighteen-mile drive to Kendall over a wide, well-built highway, through clouds of suffocating dust. "This is nothing," said Mr. Hammond. "In a real dust storm you can't see a foot ahead. I've gone up to Lakin and had to stay two days because of not being able to see the road. If a storm overtakes one on the road all one can do is to park at the side, pull up the windows and wait."

"Where are all the prairie dogs?" I asked.

"Poisoned every dog in Hamilton County—had to, they were so destructive," he replied. "Rattlers, bull snakes, and coyotes are still with us, but the wolves are gone."

For a while we rode along in silence, no sound save the mournful swish of the dust-laden wind as it surged intermittently over the desolate waste, setting tumbleweeds in motion and ruffling the young silver-gray plumes of the sagebrush.

How often in that long-ago time I had stood at my window in the early morning and watched the play of the wind among the sagebrush— and thought of the waves breaking on a distant Atlantic beach, and of how well chosen were the words lettered by my uncle on the walls of the breakfast room in our summer home—"The morning wind forever blows: the poem of creation is uninterrupted." Uninterruptedly it blows today over miles of sagebrush, as it blew in Coronado's day, as it has blown since the dawn of creation.

My meditation was broken by the strange appearance on the road of a dog team of huskies pulling a sort of gypsy van. Beside it walked two sunburned men who said they were "mushing" to Colorado Springs.

Following and speeding past them came the palatial transcontinental bus. If only an airplane had passed over, progressive stages of transportation would have been visualized.

I cannot properly picture the desolation of that ride in the little Ford, through the dust-laden air, over the prairie, apparently as tenantless of wild as of human life.

"One interesting feature of the dust storms," Mr. Hammond remarked, "is that thousands of Indian relics have been uncovered."

"Were it not for the AAA and the CCC western Kansas would be ruined,"[2] said he. "Thousands of young men just out of school, willing to work, found no opening anywhere. What happened? They took to the road. Every day some were at our back door to earn a meal. Hundreds landed here on freight cars. The railroad men said there were too many to try to kick off, so they let them ride. Now they are in CCC camps. As for the AAA, it has bought our poor starved cattle, lent us money, and enabled us to go on with renewed courage."

Kendall Cemetery, on the brow of a bluff, was surrounded by a barbed-wire fence. This was the plot I used to dread seeing because of wolf borings. I noticed many of the graves were cemented like small tombs.

From this cheerless spot, we drove rapidly down into what remained of Kendall. There were a few stores, wide distances apart, with dingy, fly-specked stock, and maybe twenty-five dwellings of all sorts and conditions, the inevitable dark red boardinghouse, a good-sized railway station, and an ugly, great black building with a huge sign, "Lumberyard." I went to a nearby shack and asked if that building occupied the site of the Chicago Lumber Company of Kansas. I was told that it did. It was in one corner of that old building that I began my Kendall experience. From the lumberyard, we drove over the drifted prairie road, along which, in 1886, rolled thousands of covered wagons. The sagebrush grew on either side, thick as moss.

Surely the tiny stone house set in the midst of sand drift, ashes, and debris could not be the pretty cottage my father built and to which he took me with such pride; I peered through the windows into the tenantless interior. In the dining room the open fireplace was blocked up and covered with wallpaper. On the floor of the living room were inches of dirt. The two sheds were still intact. In one of these I kept my prairie dog and his companion, the owl. No improvements had been made and apparently no repairs. The shingles on the roof were shredding; the cistern with top torn off was a menace; all around the house were dunes of sand.

I could not linger to investigate further, and we turned our backs on Kendall and drove across the decaying wooden bridge that spans the Arkansas, now dried to a thread, and went into the sand hills of the great American desert, where the only sign of human life was a battered and broken-down Conestoga wagon.

At the age of three score years and ten the law of the City of Boston called for my retirement from the Boston Public Library. In looking ahead, all my plans had been made with regard to the things my dearly beloved comrade and I would do together, but before that time came Edith had passed into the next life. After nearly forty years of closest companionship, I was left to face retirement alone, never doubting, however, that she still lived vitally and radiantly beyond this bourne of Time and Place.

The first years of my retirement passed somewhat slowly. My days were fully occupied, but I missed the work that had claimed my attention for forty years; and when people said, as they frequently did, "How wonderful it must be to have time for the things you have always wanted to do," I could only reply, "The things I have been doing for most of my life were the things I wanted to do."

On 8 December 1941, when I took in the morning paper, I read these startling headlines: "Japan strikes all over the Pacific. On Hawaii, Guam, Philippines, takes heavy toll. Sea battle on. Many Americans killed in Hawaii by Japanese bombs."

A few hours later in the evening edition, the headlines announced: "Congress votes war." My first thought was, now as in the last war, my time belongs to my country. I had no doubt that the club I had served in 1917 could use me. The service card given me to sign specified that women over sixty were not needed. Nothing daunted, I applied at four other service organizations. At each of these my age made me an undesirable. I knit socks, sewed buttons on little garments, and did any odd jobs that came my way.

After two months of being "undesirable," I joined a group of young, active women who were attending a course on how to run a war information service. As a sort of curiosity among all these young persons, a news photographer spotted me and my picture got into the daily newspaper. It was seen by a young librarian who was conducting a library service for the Massachusetts Committee on Public Safety. He telephoned and asked if I would help him.

Next day I had luncheon with him. He tactfully told me how much I

Edith Guerrier, in old age, in her apartment in the Nottingham Hill house that contained the Paul Revere Pottery works, Brighton, Massachusetts. Note that the fireplace tiles and pottery are Paul Revere pieces. Reproduced courtesy of the Whaling Museum, New Bedford, Massachusetts.

reminded him of his grandmother, who was still very spry, and said he would be so glad if I would volunteer a few hours a week. A few hours soon became a few days. The few days became weeks, and soon I was on duty from 9 A.M. until 5 P.M., five days a week.

After a few months the efficient and resourceful young librarian was offered so responsible and interesting a "paid defense job" elsewhere that he left, and I inherited the task of being librarian to the Massachusetts Committee on Public Safety.

As far back as October 1774, a committee on public safety had existed. It was chosen at that time to consider what was necessary for the safety of the Province of Massachusetts. From 20 October 1774, a committee on public safety operated until July 1775, when its place was taken by councillors and committees appointed by the legislature.

On 9 February 1917, nearly two months before the United States declared war on Germany—2 April 1917—Governor McCall of Massachusetts,[3] foreseeing that war for the United States was inevitable, appointed one hundred citizens chosen from every section of the Commonwealth as a "Committee on Public Safety." This committee continued until 20 November 1918, when it was dissolved. Its object had been "to secure protection from foreign aggression and insure against treachery and violence within the state." Twenty-two years later on 25 August 1940, Governor Saltonstall[4] appointed a committee on public safety consisting of one hundred and fifty representative citizens, to make plans to meet situations that might arise from war or threat of war.

At the time of which I write, the Committee on Public Safety occupied several floors in an office building, one side of which abutted on King's Chapel burying ground, where many of the earliest citizens of Boston are buried. It was the business of the library to collect, file, classify, and distribute information on methods that had proved effective in dealing with actual disaster, on analyses by technical experts, on the various types of bombs, gases, and structural defense, and on blackouts and evacuation.

In the late spring of 1945, with the end of World War II in Europe, the library files were turned over to the Commonwealth. On arrival at the State Library, they became archives. The room which had for several years been the library of the Massachusetts Committee on Public Safety was no longer a library; it was an office to let, and I was without a job.

EPILOGUE,

1945–1950

 When retired from active service, one has a strong urge to find new adventure. One day, as I had stood looking at the old King's Chapel burying ground, I became aware of how little I knew of the men and women whose venerated names were fast becoming obliterated on the lichen-covered stones of our old graveyards. To one who cannot venture far afield, the study of local history is a worthwhile occupation; to become acquainted with the lives of those individuals who were the founders of this Commonwealth is a rewarding pursuit; and the acquiring of books written by and about them is a proper task for an ex-librarian.

Not ten minutes from the headquarters of the Massachusetts Committee on Public Safety are Cornhill and Brattle streets, known as the streets of antique books. I soon discovered that tracing the whereabouts of procurable writings by our "founding fathers" called for the intuition of a Sherlock Holmes, as well as the nose of a book-hound. The volumes I sought could not always be found in bookstores. I have stumbled upon desired items in an old barn in the suburbs and in a mouldy cellar in the Back Bay.

Recalling Grandfather's great admiration for Bartholomew Gosnold,[1] I tried without success to procure reprints of the narratives of Archer and Brereton,[2] his companions on the voyage to Cuttyhunk. I am still looking for reprints. In the meantime, I have given first place to Daniel Ricketson's *History of New Bedford*,[3] in which appear extracts from both Archer's and Brereton's tales. On page 122 of this history is Daniel Ricketson's suggestion for the "round tower built of stone in a rude but substantial manner," which now marks the spot upon which the first building on the New England coast was erected by Englishmen in 1602.

The second item to be placed upon my shelves was a reprint of Captain John Smith's last literary effort, published the year of his death in 1631.[4] There was nothing puritanical about Captain Smith. His experiences had prepared him to be governor of Virginia and admiral of New England. He came to America a well-traveled soldier who had fought in France, in the "low countries," and in Turkey where he had been captured and sold as a slave. He escaped and wandered as far as Russia. Of that country, he commented, "I met with more respect, worth, content and entertainment than I had ever known in my life and not any Governor where I came but gave somewhat as a present besides my charges, seeing themselves as subject to the like calamity."

My next acquisition was a reprint of William Bradford's *History of Plymouth Plantation*, published by the Commonwealth of Massachusetts after the return to the United States in 1898 of Bradford's manuscript, which had been lost for several hundred years and was discovered in the library of the Bishop of London.

Of the books I have collected up to the present time, I shall mention but two more—the first being John Winthrop's *History of New England*. In vain I also sought some writing by one of our most eminent English founders, John Harvard. Not the smallest scrap of his writings endured. I then tried to obtain a list of the four hundred books he had given to Harvard University. After following many deceptive leads, I found a copy, and beneath the author entry, "John Downame. The Christian Warfare Against the Deuill World and Flesh," was penciled, "Escaped when the library was burnt." This is said to be the only volume left of the original gift.

On my bookshelves were now over one thousand items telling the story of New England from 1602 to 1900. What library, I wondered, would welcome the collection as a gift? New England had in its great libraries the finest collections in the world of New England literature. The Pacific coast libraries were not so well equipped. After a brief survey I offered the books to the library of Lewis and Clark College in Portland, Oregon. Its president graciously accepted the gift and thither the books went.

I know some other worthwhile task is just around the corner, and I am waiting eagerly to welcome it.

In the meantime, along came the birthday that recorded my fourscore years, and also the fifty-first anniversary of the library story-hour group. The members of that first group and members of succeeding groups gathered, some even flying from Oregon and Ohio, as well as from Vermont and all parts of Massachusetts. It was an interesting gathering—Italy, Russia, Poland, France, Germany, and England were all represented by American citizens. As I blew out the lighted candles representing the years on the anniversary cake, I knew that while the flames might be blown out, the happy memories of the years would never be extinguished.*

* Edith Guerrier died in 1958 at the age of eighty-eight.—ED.

NOTES

Foreword

1. For the "New Woman," see Dorothy M. Brown, *Setting a Course* (Boston: Twayne Publishers, 1987), 29–31. For education, see Barbara Miller Solomon, *In the Company of Educated Women* (New Haven: Yale University Press, 1985), 62–66.
2. For the importance of the support lesbian women gave each other in the settlement house movement, see Blanche Wiesen Cook. "Female Support Networks and Political Activism," reprinted in Nancy F. Cott and Elizabeth H. Pleck. *A Heritage of Her Own* (New York: Simon and Schuster, 1979), 412–44.
3. For a good discussion of the way women improvise their lives rather than working toward a defined goal, see Mary Catherine Bateson, *Composing a Life* (New York: Atlantic Monthly Press, 1989).
4. *S.E.G. News* (January 1952): 28–29, Research Library, Boston Public Library. For similarities between the library clubs and the Working Girls' Club movement of the same period, see Joanne Reitano, "Working Girls Unite," *American Quarterly* 36 (Spring 1984): 112–34. For a discussion of "immigrant gifts," see Eileen Boris, *Art and Labor: Ruskin, Morris, and the Craftsman Ideal in America* (Philadelphia: Temple University Press, 1986, 131–34, and Jane Addams, *Twenty Years at Hull House* (New York: Macmillan Co., 1910; reprint, Signet edition, 1961), 171–78.
5. Walter Muir Whitehill, *The Boston Public Library: A Centennial History* (Cambridge, Mass.: Harvard University Press, 1956), 164, 182. When Alice M. Jordan became the second custodian of the Boston Public Library's children's room in 1902, she brought Marie Shedlock of London to introduce storytelling formally as a library activity. See Alice M. Jordan, "The Library Story Hour," *S.E.G. News* 3 (18 May 1915): 3–4; Gail Eaton, "Alice M. Jordan," in Marilyn L. Miller, ed., *Dictionary of Pioneers and Leaders in Library Services to Youth* (Littleton, Colo.: Libraries Unlimited, forthcoming).
6. For the concept of how women entered new fields using innovation, see Penina Migdal Glazer and Miriam Slater, *Unequal Colleagues: The Entrance of Women into the Professions, 1890–1940* (New Brunswick, N.J.: Rutgers University Press, 1987), 217–

19. For a history of women and librarianship in this period, see Dee Garrison, *Apostles of Culture: The Public Librarian and American Society, 1876–1920* (New York: Free Press, 1979), 206–25. Garrison, however, misses the genuine response of the children to the children's rooms and their programs as well as slighting librarians' efforts to stock books in the language of their patrons. For an explanation of how women later were kept from advancing in the new careers as they became professionalized, see, for librarians, Garrison, 226–35; and for settlement house workers, see Judith Ann Trolander, *Professionalism and Social Change* (New York: Columbia University Press, 1987), 31–67.

7. *S.E.G. News* (January 1952): 5–6.

8. For a discussion of the Arts and Crafts movement as it was translated in America, see Boris, *Art and Labor*, and Wendy Kaplan, *"The Art that is Life": The Arts and Crafts Movement in America, 1876–1920* (Boston: Museum of Fine Arts, 1987).

9. "Story of the Paul Revere Pottery," *Craftsman* 25 (October 1913): 205–7.

10. Edith Guerrier, "A Brief Survey of the L.C.H. Groups," *S.E.G. News* 3 (14 November 1914): 5–6.

11. Ibid.; Celia Goodman Stern, "The Pottery," in *The Story of the Saturday Evening Girls* (Boston, 1919), 8; "The Paul Revere Pottery," *S.E.G. News* 4 (11 December 1915): 3; *Tricentennial Exhibition of The Society of Arts & Crafts* (Boston: Museum of Fine Arts, 1 March to 20 March 1917), 23; Kaplan, *"The Art that is Life,"* 30, 312–13; interview with Barbara Kramer, daughter of SEG member, Ethel Epstein Maysles, 13 November 1990, Boston. In addition to memorabilia on the Saturday Evening Girls, Barbara Kramer and her husband, Bernard, have an outstanding collection of the Paul Revere pottery. In 1912 the average woman Boston Public Library worker earned eight dollars a week, while a librarian with skills and some advanced education earned between twelve and fifteen dollars a week. *Boston Public Library Annual Report*, No. 61, 1912–13, p. 28. For the length of the work week, see Alice Kessler Harris, *Out to Work: A History of Wage-Earning Women in the United States* (New York: Oxford University Press, 1982), 198–205.

12. *S.E.G. News* 5 (June 1917): 12. For an explanation of the separatist approach, see Glazer and Slater, *Unequal Colleagues*, 219–22. For discussions of the ideas and attitudes of women in the settlement house movement, see Mina Carson, *Settlement Folk: Social Thought and the American Settlement Movement, 1885–1930* (Chicago: University of Chicago Press, 1990), 101–21, and Trolander, 7–24. For Denison House, see Carson, 79–80, 95; Allen F. Davis, "Helena Stuart Dudley," in *Notable American Women* (Cambridge, Mass.: Harvard University Press, 1971), vol. 1: 526–27, hereafter cited as *NAW*; and Theresa Corcoran, "Vida Scudder," in *NAW, The Modern Period*, 636–37. For the Boston Women's Trade Union League, see Stephen H. Norwood, *Labor's Flaming Youth: Telephone Operators and Worker Militancy, 1878–1923* (Urbana: University of Illinois Press, 1990), 90–122.

13. Geoffrey Blodgett, "Pauline Agassiz Shaw," *NAW*, vol. 3: 278–80; Sharon Hartman Strom, "Leadership and Tactics in the American Woman Suffrage Movement: A New Perspective from Massachusetts," *Journal of American History* 62 (September 1975): 296–315; Leonard Ware, *Helen Osborne Storrow 1864–1944: A Memoir* (Northampton, Mass., 1970). James Jackson Storrow was defeated by John F. Fitzgerald in a mayoralty election in 1905. Although Bostonian Margaret Deland saw herself as a new

woman, she opposed women's suffrage because she did not want to add unprepared women to the company of men she believed were not qualified, yet who were already voting. Margaret Deland, "The Change in the Feminine Ideal," *Atlantic Monthly* 105, March 1910, 291–93; idem., *Golden Yesterdays* (New York: Harper Bros., 1940), 289–90.

14. *S.E.G. News* (January 1952): 27.

15. For a report on the futures of the SEG members, see *S.E.G. News* (January 1952), and *S.E.G. News*, Cherry Tree Edition, 1954. For the book fund, see *S.E.G. News* (January 1952): 5.

16. Lucy Larcom, *A New England Girlhood* (1889; reprint, Gloucester, Mass.: Peter Smith, 1973); Lucy Maud Montgomery, *Anne of Green Gables* (1908; reprint, New York: Grosset & Dunlap, 1970); Johanna Spyri, *Heidi* (1880; reprint, Racine, Wisc.: Whitman Publishing, 1965).

17. For a discussion of the "family claim," a concept first discussed by Jane Addams, see Joyce Antler, "'After College, What?': New Graduates and the Family Claim," *American Quarterly* 32 (Fall 1980): 409–34.

Introduction

1. Shaw, daughter of the eminent naturalist Louis Agassiz and wife of one of the richest men in Boston, Quincy Adams Shaw, was an ardent proponent of early childhood education. In 1877 she opened kindergartens in the Boston suburb of Brookline and in Jamaica Plain, a part of metropolitan Boston (by 1883 she had opened 31 of them), and the next year started organizing day nurseries in tenement districts, one of them in the North Bennet Street Industrial School, another one of her philanthropies. She was also an active supporter of vocational education.

2. Paula J. Todisco, *Boston's First Neighborhood: The North End* (Boston: Boston Public Library, 1976), 29.

3. Frederick A. Bushee, "The Invading Host," in Robert A. Woods, ed., *Americans in Process: A Settlement Study* (1903; reprint, New York: Arno, 1970), 49, 57.

4. Ibid., 62.

5. Edward H. Chandler, "City and Slum," in Woods, *Americans in Process*, 94, 99.

6. Mrs. L. E. Caswell, *Report of the North End Industrial Home, 39 North Bennet Street, from January, 1880, to April, 1881* (Boston: Frank Wood, Printer, 1881), North Bennet Street Industrial School Collection, Schlesinger Library, Radcliffe College, 16–21.

7. Laura Stanton, ed., *North Bennet Street School: A Short History 1885–1985* (Boston, 1985), 20–21.

8. "The English Conference: Official Report of Proceedings," *Library Journal* 2, nos. 5–6 (January–February 1878): 280. Quoted by Dee Garrison in her *Apostles of Culture: The Public Librarian and American Society, 1876–1920* (New York: Free Press, 1979), 175.

9. Edith Guerrier, "The Little Woman's Forebears," in her *A Little Woman of New England*, MS, Ricketson Collection, Old Dartmouth Historical Society, New Bedford, Mass., 3.

10. The Isle of Dogs, once a peninsula on the north side of the Thames River, became an island when the West India Dock Canal was dug from Limehouse to Blackwall during the nineteenth century.

11. George Guerrier, notes on his ancestry, Ricketson Collection.

12. George Guerrier, "Record of Military Service," Ricketson Collection. Copy.

13. John V. DeGrasse, Discharge Certificate for George Guerrier, Ricketson Collection. Copy.

14. Joseph Ricketson to George Guerrier, 19 May 1865, Ricketson Collection.

15. Emma Guerrier to George, 12 September 1871, Ricketson Collection.

16. Receipt for land, 22 February 1872, Ricketson Collection.

17. Emma Guerrier to George, 28 April 1872, Ricketson Collection.

18. "Rev. Samuel Fox," Methodist Episcopal Church, Conferences, New England Southern. *Official Journal and Yearbook of the New England Southern Conference of the Methodist Episcopal Church*, 64th Session, New Bedford, Mass., 23–28 March 1904, 100–102.

19. "Ninety Years," *New Bedford Evening Standard*, 20 July 1903, 6.

20. George Guerrier to Edith, 6 February 1890, Ricketson Collection.

21. George Guerrier to Edith, 27 February 1890, Ricketson Collection.

22. Eldon Hubert Martin, *Vermont College: A Famous Old School* (Nashville: Parthenon Press, 1962), 170.

23. George Guerrier to Edith, 3 November 1891, Ricketson Collection.

24. George Guerrier to Edith, 4 December 1891, Ricketson Collection.

25. Boston Public Library, *Annual Report #48*, 1899–1900, 54.

26. Walton Ricketson, diary, entry for 14 March 1906, Ricketson Collection.

27. Edith Guerrier to George, undated, Ricketson Collection.

28. George Guerrier to Edith, 11 June 1906, Ricketson Collection.

29. George Guerrier's death certificate, signed by W. Franklin Wood, M.D., Director of McLean Hospital, certifies that Guerrier, admitted 8 April 1907 with a diagnosis of arteriosclerotic dementia, died 13 April 1911.

30. He saw five volumes of his verse into print: *The Classic Farmer; and Other Poems* (New Bedford, Mass., 1869), *Pipes of Corn* (Boston: W. P. Clarke, 1880), *A Lodge in the Wilderness* (Boston: Franklin Press, Rand Avery & Co., 1883), *The Giovanni* (Montpelier, Vt., 1889), and *Greens and Yellows* (Boston: Press of S. J. Parkhill, 1900).

31. George Guerrier, notes on his ancestry, Ricketson Collection.

32. Edith Guerrier (probable author), Paper on the Saturday Evening Girls and their pottery, n.d., Ricketson Collection.

33. *S.E.G. News* (11 December 1915): 2.

34. "Edith Brown," *Boston Transcript*, 2 September 1932, photocopy.

35. William Lloyd Garrison II to George Guerrier, 27 November 1901, MS 1490, no. 78, Boston Public Library.

36. Leonard Ware, *Helen Osborne Storrow 1864–1944: A Memoir* (Northampton, Mass.: 1970), 11–12.

37. Guerrier, "A Brief Survey of the L.C.H. Groups," *S.E.G. News* (14 November 1914): 5–6.

38. North Bennet Street Industrial School, *Annual Report #40*, 1905–06, 7; *Annual Report #41*, 1906–07, 9; *Annual Report #42*, 1908–09, 28.

39. Barbara Solomon, *In the Company of Educated Women* (New Haven: Yale University Press, 1985), 64.

40. *S.E.G. News* (Cherry Tree Edition, 1954): 15.

1   A Motherless Child

1. Aunt Fanny was Frances Thornton Ricketson, wife of Daniel Ricketson's younger brother Joseph.
2. Rollo, the central character of a series of books by Jacob Abbott (1803–1879), is a small boy learning to talk and read.
3. The seven little sisters were characters in a frequently reprinted book by Jane Andrews, *The Seven Little Sisters Who Live on the Round Ball that Floats in the Air* (Boston: Ticknor and Fields, 1861).
4. Patmore's anthology, originally published in 1862, included both John Keats's "La Belle Dame sans Merci" and Sir Walter Scott's "Young Lochinvar."
5. William Wall (1801–1885) was a painter of some local reputation in New England whose output included narrative paintings, landscapes, and portraits. He was a close friend of Daniel Ricketson.
6. Henry David Thoreau, *Walden* (New York: Modern Library, 1937), 76.
7. Uncle Fox actually remained in each pulpit about two years, except for six years at the Seamen's Bethel in New Bedford.
8. Edith should have answered with her own name or names, which is the answer indicated by the *N* and *M* printed in the catechism.
9. The Musketaquid is better known as the Concord River.
10. *Hans Brinker* . . . (1865) was a popular children's novel written by Mary Mapes Dodge.
11. Henry Wadsworth Longfellow's poem was a standard elocution exercise for many decades.
12. A democrat wagon is a light, horse-drawn farm wagon with one or two seats.
13. Charles Freeman, a convert to a splinter sect of the Methodist Church called the Adventists, became convinced that he was called upon by God to sacrifice his child as Abraham had agreed to sacrifice Isaac. Accordingly, late on the night of 30 April 1879, he stabbed her with a sheath knife, firm in his belief—which he shared with his wife and other members of the sect—that the child would revive after three days' time. When the little girl did not return to life, Freeman's wife first began to doubt, and then repent; she was not held. Her husband was judged not guilty by reason of insanity, and was remanded to an asylum. (*Boston Globe*, 3 May 1879, 1; 4 May 1879, 1; 6 May 1879, 1; 18 October 1879, 4; 30 January 1880, 2.)
14. According to the *Boston City Directory* for the relevant period, Aunt Fanny's house was not on Harrison Avenue, but at 29 Marcella Avenue.

2   Father and Daughter

1. "The Blue Juniata" is the title of a song written by Marion D. Sullivan, probably about the Juniata River, which flows through central Pennsylvania.
2. Merdle, a character in Charles Dickens's *Little Dorritt*, was a swindling financier.
3. *Lalla Rookh*, a sequence of oriental verses connected by a prose story, was written by Thomas Moore (1779–1852) and first published in 1817.
4. "Lotta" was Charlotte Crabtree (1847–1924), an American actress famous for her performances in burlesques and other spectacular productions.
5. Cibola, a collection of Zuni Indian villages in western New Mexico, was a place of

fabulous wealth, according to the report of an envoy of Mexico's Spanish viceroy in 1539. The following year the Spanish conquistador Francisco Vásquez de Coronado y Valdes set out to find it. He failed, but did explore a vast amount of previously uncharted territory between Mexico and Kansas.

6. Count de Charney, the hero of *Picciola*, a novel by S. B. Saintine first published in 1836, was a prisoner who drew comfort from his love for a small plant, the picciola, which grew in the courtyard outside his cell.

7. The narrative poem *Lucile* was published under the name of Owen Meredith, a pseudonym for Edward Robert Bulwer-Lytton, Earl of Lytton (1831–1891), who was the son of the novelist Edward Bulwer-Lytton, Baron Lytton (1803–1873).

3 A Single Woman

1. The Museum School, at this period still called by its original name, the School of Drawing and Painting, had been established to fulfill an article of the Museum's 1870 charter that specified rooms be set aside for "instruction in the fine arts." It did not become the School of the Museum of Fine Arts until October 1901.

2. An excerpt from the frequently anthologized "Spring," by Celia Thaxter (1835–1894).

3. A quotation from Charles Dickens's *Pickwick Papers*, chapter 30, "Eccentricities of genius, Sam."

4. "Lytton's romance" is *The Last Days of Pompeii* by Edward Bulwer-Lytton, Baron Lytton, first published in 1834.

5. In Shakespeare's *Merchant of Venice*, Jessica is Shylock's daughter and Lorenzo the young man with whom she elopes.

6. The "well-managed private hospital" was McLean Hospital, a psychiatric hospital in the Boston suburb of Belmont.

7. Louisa de la Rame ("Ouida"), *The Nürnberg Stove* (Boston: Joseph Knight Co., 1893), 92.

8. The North End Union, established in 1892 by the Benevolent Fraternity of Unitarian Churches, offered a number of services to North End residents, such as a milk station, public baths, and a summer camp. It also sponsored the first plumbing school in New England (1894) and the first printing school (1900).

9. The Women's Municipal League, founded in 1908, was concerned with municipal housekeeping (sanitation, waste disposal, maintenance of streets and alleys, and so on), education, and social welfare. Its members worked diligently—before and after the First World War—to help Americanize the foreign born.

10. John Francis "Honey Fitz" Fitzgerald (1863–1950), the grandfather of President John F. Kennedy, was mayor of Boston from 1906 to 1907 and from 1910 to 1914.

11. A popular song, words and music by Fred Seaver.

12. Walter Scott Lenox, an American porcelain manufacturer, established the Ceramic Art Company in Trenton in 1889 and renamed it the Lenox China Company in 1906.

13. The firm of Knowles, Taylor & Knowles, organized in 1891, began with Isaac Knowles and Isaac Taylor manufacturing porcelain and pottery in East Liverpool, Ohio, in 1854. The firm produced ironstone, semiporcelain, Belleck ware (for a short period), and Lotus ware (similar to Belleek).

14. Rookwood Pottery, founded in Cincinnati in 1880, made commercial tableware, umbrella stands, and other pottery products. It reached its peak between 1907 and 1933, but finally closed in 1967.
15. Henry Chapman Mercer (1856–1930), an anthropologist and archaeologist, first experimented with tile manufacture in Doylestown, Pennsylvania, using pottery techniques he had studied in Germany. His designs were often derived from handcrafted items like Moravian stove-plates, medieval English tiles, and Native American objects.
16. Charles Volkmar (1841–1914) studied painting in Paris and worked as a decorator for a French potter before setting up a kiln at Greenpoint, N.Y., in 1879. He later headed other potteries in Trenton and Brooklyn, N.Y., and Metuchen, N.J.
17. Adelaide Alsop Robineau (1865–1929) designed, threw, modeled, carved, and decorated pieces for the Robineau Pottery in Syracuse. In the beginning her motifs were naturalistic, then Art Nouveau, then Oriental Mayan. Her Scarab Vase won the Gran Premio at the International Exhibition in Turin in 1911.

4 On Loan to Mr. Hoover

1. Martha Evelyn Davis White was a prominent clubwoman of the period and a member of many organizations, including the Arlington Woman's Club, New England Woman's Club and the Boston Women's City Club.
2. The apron is a woman's coverall named for Herbert Hoover.
3. Householders who signed pledges to conserve food received Home Cards, which were issued in June and October of 1917 and in June 1918. A fourth set of cards, printed for distribution in December 1918, was never issued.
4. The Latrobe stove was invented by John Hazlehurst Boneval Latrobe (1801–1891), lawyer, inventor, and a founder of the Republic of Liberia.
5. William Gibbs McAdoo (1863–1941), a Tennessee lawyer, was secretary of the treasury during Woodrow Wilson's administration, and also chairman of the Federal Reserve Board, the Federal Farm Loan Board, and the War Finance Corporation, as well as director general of the railroads after their takeover by the government in 1917.
6. In *We Pledged Allegiance* (p. 160), Guerrier told this story about a "Mr. Swenson," but no one of that name has ever governed Wisconsin. The likeliest candidate as hero of the tale is James O. Davidson (1854–1922), born in the Sogn region of Norway, who was governor of Wisconsin from 1906 to 1911.
7. A newspaperman, Ben S. Allen was an adviser to Herbert Hoover during and after his presidency. He died in 1963 at the age of 80.
8. Philander Priestley Claxton (1862–1957) was U.S. commissioner of education from 1911 to 1921.
9. John Edward Raker (1863–1926), a Democrat from California, served in the House of Representatives of the U.S. Congress from 1911 to 1926.
10. A Republican Representative to the U.S. Congress from Massachusetts, Frederick William Dallinger (1871–1955) served from 1915 to 1925 and from 1926 to 1932.
11. David Ignatius Walsh (1872–1947) served as Senator from Massachusetts from 1919 to 1925 and from 1926 to 1947.
12. Thomas Lindsay Blanton (1872–1957) was a Democratic Representative to the U.S. Congress from 1917 to 1919 and from 1930 to 1937.

13. Reed Smoot, a Republican who served in the Senate from 1903 to 1933, was best known as the coauthor of the Smoot-Hawley Tariff Act of 1930.
14. Franklin K. Lane, *The American Spirit: Addresses in War-time* (New York: Frederick A. Stokes, 1918). Lane was Wilson's secretary of the interior from 1913 to 1920.
15. Newton Diehl Baker (1871–1937) was secretary of war in President Wilson's cabinet from 1916 to 1921.
16. William Cox Redfield (1858–1932) served as secretary of commerce to President Wilson from 1913 to 1919.
17. Charles Gates Dawes, who retained the title of brigadier general from his service with the American Expeditionary Forces in France during the First World War, was appointed first director of the U.S. Bureau of the Budget in 1921. He served as vice president of the United States from 1925 to 1929.
18. Lawrence Cowle Phipps (1862–1958), a Republican from Colorado, was chairman of the Senate Committee on Education and Labor of the Sixty-eighth and Sixty-ninth Congresses.
19. George Higgins Moses (1869–1958) was a Republican member of the U.S. Senate from 1918 to 1933.

5   A Civil Servant

1. A reference to Elbert Hubbard's essay recounting the Spanish-American War story of an American soldier dispatched to General Calixto Garcia y Iniques, head of the Cuban insurgent forces, to learn what help Garcia needed against the Spanish.
2. AAA, the Agricultural Adjustment Act, was enacted in 1933 to bring farm income into parity with national income by limiting production of basic agricultural commodities. Declared unconstitutional by the Supreme Court in 1936, it was reestablished by the Act of 1938 and subsequently amended from the 1940s to the 1960s. The CCC, the Civilian Conservation Corps, was the first New Deal agency to deal with the problem of unemployed young men. Between 1933 and 1941, three million single men from the ages of seventeen to twenty-five worked on conservation tasks like reforestation, erosion control, and land reclamation. The Corps, made obsolete by World War II, went out of existence in 1942.
3. Samuel Walker MCall (1851–1923), a Republican, was governor of Massachusetts from 1916 to 1919.
4. Leverett Saltonstall (1892–1979), a Republican, was governor of Massachusetts from 1939 to 1944.

Epilogue

1. Bartholomew Gosnold was an English navigator who, in 1602, discovered Cape Cod, Martha's Vineyard, and Elizabeth Island (now called Cuttyhunk), where he planted the first English settlement in New England. He died at the Jamestown settlement in Virginia on 22 August 1607.
2. Gabriel Archer, . . . *Gosnold's Settlement at Cuttyhunk. The Relation of Captain Gosnold's Voyage to the North Part of Virginia, Begun the Six-and-twentieth of March, Anno 42, Elizabethae Reginae, 1602, and Delivered by Gabriel Archer, a Gentleman in the Said Voyage*

(Boston: Directors of the Old South Work, 1902). John Brereton, *A Briefe and True Relation of the Discouerie of the North Part of Virginia; Being a Most Pleasant, Fruitfull and Commodious Soile: Made This Present Year 1602, by Captaine Bartholomew Gosnold, Captaine Bartholomew Gilbert, and Diuers Other Gentlemen Their Associates.* . . . (London, 1602).

3. Daniel Ricketson, *History of New Bedford, Bristol County, Massachusetts.* . . . (New Bedford: Published by the author, 1858).

4. John Smith, *Advertisement for the Unexperienced Planters of New-England, or Anywhere, or the Path-way to Experience to Build a Plantation.* . . . (London: printed by I. Haviland and are to be sold by R. Milbourne, 1631).

SELECT

BIBLIOGRAPHY

Collections

North Bennet Street Industrial School Collection. Schlesinger Library, Radcliffe College, Cambridge, Mass.
Ricketson Collection. Old Dartmouth Historical Society. New Bedford Whaling Museum Library, New Bedford, Mass.

Primary and Secondary Sources

Antler, Joyce. "'After College, What?': New Graduates and the Family Claim." *American Quarterly* 32 (Fall 1980): 409–34.
Blaxall, Martha, and Barbara Reagan, eds. *Women and the Workplace: The Implications of Occupational Segregation.* Chicago: University of Chicago Press, 1976.
Blodgett, Geoffrey. "Pauline Agassiz Shaw." In *Notable American Women 1607–1950: A Biographical Dictionary,* vol. 3: 278–80. Cambridge, Mass.: Belknap Press of Harvard University Press, 1971.
Boston, Mass. Public Library. Board of Trustees. *Annual Reports.* Nos. 45–67 (1896–1918).
Bowker, R.R. "Women in the Library Profession." *Library Journal* 45 (15 June 1920): 545–49; (1–15 July 1920): 587–92; (August 1920): 635–40.
Brand, Barbara E. "Librarianship and Other Female Intensive Professions." *Journal of Library History* 18 (Fall 1983): 391–406.
Brindisi, Rocco. "The Italian and Public Health." *Charities* 12 (1904): 483–504.
Britton, Jasmine. "The Library's Share in Americanization." *Library Journal* 43 (October 1918): 723–27.
Brugh, Ann E., and Benjamin R. Beede. "American Librarianship." *Signs* 1 (Summer 1976): 943–55.
Cameron, Elisabeth. *Encyclopedia of Pottery & Porcelain 1800–1960.* New York: Facts on File, 1986.

Carson, Mina. *Settlement Folk: Social Thought and the American Settlement Movement, 1885–1930.* Chicago: University of Chicago Press, 1990.

"Character of Italian Immigration." *New England Magazine* n.s.35 (1906): 216–20.

Chiles, Robert E. *Theological Transition in American Methodism: 1790–1935.* New York: Abingdon Press, 1965.

Conway, Jill. "Women Reformers and American Culture, 1870–1930." *Journal of Social History* 5 (Winter 1971–72): 164–77.

Cutler, Mary S. "What a Woman Librarian Earns." *Library Journal* 18 (August 1892): 89–91.

Dain, Phyllis. "Ambivalence and Paradox: The Social Bonds of the Public Library." *Library Journal* 100 (1 February 1975): 261–66.

Dana, John Cotton. "Hear the Other Side." *Library Journal* Conference of Librarians Supplement 21 (1896): 1–5.

———. "Women in Library Work." *Independent* 71 (3 August 1911): 244–50.

Davies, David William. *Public Libraries as Cultural and Social Centers: The Origin of the Concept.* Metuchen, N.J.: Scarecrow, 1974.

Davis, Allen F. *Spearheads for Reform: The Social Settlement and the Progressive Movement 1890–1914.* New York: Oxford University Press, 1967.

Davis, W. H. "The Relation of the Foreign Population to the Mortality Rates of Boston." Paper read at the 37th Annual Meeting of the American Academy of Medicine, June 1912.

"Death of Rev. Samuel Fox, an Aged Methodist Minister." *New Bedford Evening Standard,* 20 July 1903, 2.

DeMarco, William M. *Ethnics and Enclaves: Boston's Italian North End.* Ann Arbor, Mich.: UMI Research Press, 1981.

Ditzion, Sidney. *Arsenals of a Democratic Culture: A Social History of the American Public Library Movement in New England and the Middle States from 1850 to 1900.* Chicago: American Library Association, 1947.

Douglas, Ann. *The Feminization of American Culture.* New York: Alfred A. Knopf, 1977.

Driscoll, Cornelius Robert. *Daniel Ricketson and the "Shanty Society."* Master's thesis, Providence College, Rhode Island, 1977.

Edes, Grace Williamson. *William Ricketson and His Descendants.* 3 vols. Boston: Privately printed, 1917–82.

Fairchild, [Mary] Salome Cutler. "Women in American Libraries." *Library Journal* 29 (December 1904): 157–62.

Garrison, Dee. *Apostles of Culture: The Public Librarian and American Society, 1876–1920.* New York: Free Press, 1979.

———. "The Tender Technicians: The Feminization of Public Librarianship, 1876–1905." *Journal of Social History* 6 (1972–73): 131–59.

———. "Women in Libraries." In Sidney L. Jackson, Eleanor B. Herling, and E. J. Josey, eds. *A Century of Service: Librarianship in the United States and Canada,* 146–68. Chicago: American Library Association, 1976.

Green, Martin. *The Problem of Boston: Some Readings in Cultural History.* New York: W. W. Norton, 1966.

Guerrier, Edith. "The Branches of the Boston Public Library." *More Books, Being the Bulletin of the Boston Public Library* 2 (September 1927): 209–10.

————, comp. *The Federal Executive Departments as Sources of Information for Libraries.* Department of the Interior, Bureau of Education, Bulletin no. 74. Washington, D.C.: Government Printing Office, 1919.

————. *Wanderfolk in Wonderland.* Boston: Small, Maynard & Co., 1903.

————. *We Pledged Allegiance, a Librarian's Intimate Story of the United States Food Administration.* Leland Stanford Junior University. The Hoover Library of War, Revolution, and Peace. Miscellaneous Publication no. 1. Palo Alto, Calif.: Stanford University Press, 1941.

Guerrier, George P. *Kansas in a Nutshell.* Cambridge, Mass.: Printed at the Riverside Press, 1889.

————. *Pipes of Corn: A Collection of Miscellaneous Verse.* Boston: W. P. Clarke, 1880.

————. "To a Bluebird." *Harper's Magazine* 60, May 1880, 934.

Harris, Michael H. *The Purpose of the American Public Library in Historical Perspective: A Revisionist Interpretation.* Washington, D.C.: ERIC Clearinghouse on Library and Information Science, 1972.

Harris, Michael H., and Donald G. Davis, Jr. *American Library History: A Bibliography.* Austin: University of Texas Press, 1978.

Hasse, Adelaide R. "Women in Libraries." *Association of Collegiate Alumnae. Journal* 10 (October 1917): 73–80.

Hill, Joseph A. *Women in Gainful Occupations, 1870–1920.* Census Monograph 9. 1929. Reprint. Westport, Conn.: Greenwood Press, 1978.

Ingalls, Sheffield. *History of Atchison County, Kansas.* Lawrence, Kans.: Standard Publishing Co., 1916.

Jevons, W. Stanley. "The Rationale of Free Public Libraries." *Contemporary Review* 39 (1881): 385–402.

Kelso, Tessa L. "Some Economical Features of Public Libraries." *The Arena* 7 (1893): 709–13.

Kennedy, Albert J. *The Zone of Emergence: Observations of the Lower Middle and Upper Working Class Communities of Boston, 1905–1914.* 2d ed., abridged. Cambridge, Mass.: MIT Press, 1969.

King, James Ernest. "Edith Guerrier." *Bulletin of Bibliography* 18 (May–August 1943): 1–3.

Kovel, Ralph, and Terry Kovel. *The Kovels' Collector's Guide to American Art Pottery.* New York: Crown, 1974.

Kugler, Richard C. *William Allen Wall, an artist of New Bedford.* New Bedford, Mass.: Old Dartmouth Historical Society, 1978.

Lee, Robert Ellis. *Continuing Education for Adults through the American Public Library 1833–1964.* Chicago: American Library Association, 1966.

Leypoldt, Augusta H., and George Iles, eds. *List of Books for Girls and Women and Their Clubs.* Boston: The Library Bureau, 1895.

Lord, R. H. *History of the Archdiocese of Boston.* 3 vols. New York: Sheed and Ward, 1944.

MacDonald, Edward. *Old Copp's Hill and Burial Ground with Historical Sketches.* Boston: Industrial School Press, 1898.

Martin, Eldon Hubert. *Vermont College: A Famous Old School.* Nashville, Tenn.: Parthenon Press, 1962.

Methodist Episcopal Church. Conferences. New England Southern. *Official Journal and Yearbook of the New England Southern Annual Conference. . . .* Providence, R.I., 1890–1904.

Methodist Episcopal Church. Conferences. Providence. *Minutes of the Sessions, 1845–1877.* Providence, R.I., 1845–1877.

"Ninety years." *New Bedford Evening Standard,* 20 July 1903, 6.

Pearson, Henry Greenleaf. *Son of New England: James Jackson Storrow 1864–1926.* Boston: Privately printed, 1932.

Peck, A. L. "Workingmen's Clubs and the Public Library." *Library Journal* 23 (1898): 612–14.

Putnam, Herbert. "The Woman in the Library." *Library Journal* 41 (December 1916): 879–81.

Reitano, Joanne. "Working Girls Unite." *American Quarterly* 36 (Spring 1984): 112–34.

Ricketson, Anna, and Walton Ricketson, eds. *Daniel Ricketson and His Friends: Letters, Poems, Sketches, Etc.* Boston: Houghton, Mifflin and Co., 1902.

Ricketson, Daniel. *Daniel Ricketson: Autobiographic and Miscellaneous.* Ed. Anna Ricketson and Walton Ricketson. New Bedford, Mass.: E. Anthony and Sons, Inc., 1910.

Roe, Catherine, and Bill Roe, comp. *Atchison Centennial, June 20–26, 1854–1954; A Historic Album of Atchison, Kansas.* Atchison, 1954.

S.E.G. News: The Official Library Clubhouse Paper Published by the Saturday Evening Girls. 1912–1917; Supplement, January 1952, Cherry Tree Edition, 1954.

Shera, Jesse H. *Foundations of the Public Library: The Origins of the Public Library Movement in New England 1692–1855.* Chicago: University of Chicago Press, 1949.

Smith-Rosenberg, Carroll. "The Female World of Love and Ritual: Relations between Women in Nineteenth-Century America." *Signs* 1 (1975): 1–29.

Sochen, June. *Movers and Shakers: American Women Thinkers and Activists 1900–1970.* New York: Quadrangle/New York Times Book Co., 1973.

Solomon, Barbara Miller. *Ancestors and Immigrants: A Changing New England Tradition.* Cambridge, Mass.: Harvard University Press, 1956.

———. *In the Company of Educated Women: A History of Women and Higher Education in America.* New Haven: Yale University Press, 1985.

Stanton, Laura, ed. *North Bennet Street School: A Short History 1885–1985.* Boston, 1985.

Stewart, Cora. "Libraries in Relation to Settlement Work." *Library Journal* 31 (August 1906): 82–85.

Todisco, Paula J. *Boston's First Neighborhood: The North End.* Boston: Boston Public Library, 1976.

Vicinus, Martha. *Independent Women: Work and Community for Single Women 1850–1920.* Chicago: University of Chicago Press, 1985.

Wadlin, Horace G. *The Public Library of the City of Boston: A History.* Boston: Printed at the Library and published by the Trustees, 1911.

Ware, Leonard. *Helen Osborne Storrow 1864–1944: A Memoir.* Northampton, Mass., 1970.

Whitehill, Walter Muir. *The Boston Public Library: A Centennial History.* Cambridge, Mass., Harvard University Press, 1956.

———. *Museum of Fine Arts, Boston: A Centennial History.* 2 vols. Cambridge, Mass.: Belknap Press of Harvard University Press, 1970.

Whyte, William Foote. "Race Conflicts in the North End of Boston." *New England Quarterly* 12 (December 1939): 623–42.

Wieder, Arnold A. *The Early Jewish Community of Boston's North End.* Waltham, Mass.: Brandeis University, 1962.

Winger, Howard W. "American Library History: 1876–1976." *Library Trends* 25 (July 1976): 1–416.

Woods, Amy. "Italians of New England." *New England Magazine* n.s. 35 (1904): 626–32.

Woods, Robert A., ed. *Americans in Process: A Settlement Study.* 1903. Reprint. New York: Arno Press, 1970.

———, ed. *The City Wilderness: A Settlement Study by Residents and Associates of the South End House.* 1898. Reprint. New York: Garrett Press, 1970.

Woods, Robert A., and Albert J. Kennedy, eds. *Young Working Girls: A Summary of Evidence from Two Thousand Social Workers.* Boston: Houghton Mifflin, 1913.

Worrell, Dorothy. *The Women's Municipal League of Boston: A History of Thirty-Five Years of Civic Endeavor.* Boston: Women's Municipal League Committee, 1943.

INDEX